Operation 'Husky' – the Sicilian Campa

Through the eyes of the squadrons of the R.A.F. Regiment

ROBIN F FINLAYSON

Acknowledgements and Copyright

The Operational Record Book sections in this book, contain public sector information licensed under the Open Government Licence v3.0.

The Operational Record Books held at The National Archives and used in this book are listed below:

AIR 29/84 - 2744 Field Squadron

AIR 29/116 – 2855/ 2856 L.A.A. Squadrons

AIR 29/117 - 2857/ 2858/ 2858 L.A.A. Squadrons

AIR 29/118 – 2862/ 2864 L.A.A. Squadrons

AIR 29/129 – 2904/ 2906 Field Squadrons

AIR 29/133 – 2925 L.A.A. Squadron

AIR 29/120 – RAF Regiment Squadrons 2852 – 2867 Appendices only

AIR 29/130 - RAF Regiment Squadrons 2900 – 2909 Appendices only

AIR29/135 - RAF Regiment Squadrons 2924 – 2935 Appendices only

Design concept, layout and illustrations by Robin F Finlayson.

Front cover picture: RAF Regiment warm themselves against an Italian winter

First published in paperback in 2017

Copyright © 2017 RFFA Ltd

All rights preserved.

Visit Robin F Finlayson's Facebook page for further series and other publication updates.

OPERATION 'HUSKY' – the Sicilian Campaign 1943

Dedication

This book is dedicated to all who have served and specifically those that paid the ultimate sacrifice in this campaign.

The records used in this book identify those that passed away and as such are listed and remembered below.

1355517	Corporal	Rogerson W.	2855 L.A.A. Squadron
1809081	Aircraftman 1st Class	Newman G.	2855 L.A.A. Squadron
976154	Leading Aircraftman	Petrie R.	2906 Field Squadron
1272583	Corporal	Cawley	2925 L.A.A. Squadron
1114987	Corporal	Corbishley	2925 L.A.A. Squadron
652775	Leading Aircraftsman	Tully	2925 L.A.A. Squadron
1450065	Leading Aircraftsman	Humphries	2925 L.A.A. Squadron
1484947	Leading Aircraftsman	Paul	2925 L.A.A. Squadron
1502683	Leading Aircraftsman	Coe	2925 L.A.A. Squadron
1350101	Leading Aircraftsman	Wilsea	2925 L.A.A. Squadron
1391605	Leading Aircraftsman	Hayden	2925 L.A.A. Squadron
1272522	Leading Aircraftsman	Rundle	2925 L.A.A. Squadron
1315638	Leading Aircraftsman	Whaley	2925 L.A.A. Squadron
	Sergeant	Ousten	2862 L.A.A. Squadron
	Leading Aircraftsman	Smith (409)	2862 L.A.A. Squadron
	Leading Aircraftsman	Witts	2862 L.A.A. Squadron
	Leading Aircraftsman	Ankell	2862 L.A.A. Squadron
1652810	Leading Aircraftsman	Nobel	2857 L.A.A. Squadron

OPERATION 'HUSKY' – the Sicilian Campaign 1943

Key Abbreviations

Abbreviation	Meaning	Abbreviation	Meaning
Rank		Flt	Flight
A/C – A.C.1	Flt	H.Q.	Headquarters
Cpl	H.Q.	I.G.	Irish Guards
F/Lt - F/L	Flight Lieutenant	MU	Maintenance Unit
F/O - FO	Flying Officer	N.A.A.F.	North African Air Force
G/Cpt	Group Captain	N.A.A.F.I.	Navy, Army, Airforce Families Institute
L.A.C.	Leading Aircraftsman	R.A.F.R.	Royal Air Force Regiment
Lt.Col.	Lieutenant Colonel	R.H.Q.	Rear Headquarters
Maj	Major	S.H.Q.	Squadron Headquarters
P/O	Pilot Officer	Sqn - Sqdn	Squadron
Sgt	Sergeant	**Other**	
S/Ldr – S/L	Squadron Leader	A/C	Aircraft
W/Cmdr	Wing Commander	A.P.	Anti-personnel
Post, appointments or positions			Cwt
A.A.D.C.	Anti-Aircraft Defence Commander	D.F.C.	Distinguishing Flying Cross
A.A.D.O.	Anti-Aircraft Defence Officer	E/A	Enemy aircraft
Adjt	Adjutant	Hy/A.A.	Heavy Anti-Aircraft
A.L.O.	Army Liaison Officer		HE
A.O.C.	Air Officer Commanding	H.M.T.	His Majesty's Troopship
C.O.	Commanding Officer	L.C.I.	Landing Craft Infantry
DR	Despatch Rider / Driver	L.C.T. (T.L.C.)	Landing Craft Tank
i/c	In Command	LG	Landing ground
I.O.	Intelligence Officer	L.S.T.	
O.C. - OC	Officer Commanding	M.C.	Military Cross
MO	Medical Orderly	MM	Military Medal
N.C.O.	Non-Commissioned Officer	M.T.	Mechanical Transport
ORs	Other Ranks	OP	Observation post
S.M.O.	Senior Medical Officer	O Group	Orders Group
Structural, unit or type		Recce	Reconnaissance
A.F.H.Q.	Air Force Headquarters	R.V. - RV	Rendez Vous
A.H.Q.	Advanced Headquarters	U/S	Unserviceable
A.M.E.S.	Air Ministry Experimental Stations	W /(R).T.	Wireless (Radio) Transmission
Bde	Brigade	**Axis Aircraft**	
Bn	Battalion	Fiat CR	Italian Fighter aircraft (Bi-plane)
Coldm/Colds	Coldstream Guards	JU 88	Junker 88 (German medium bomber)
Coy	Company	Macchi 202	Aermacchi (Italian fighter aircraft)
D.A.F.	Desert Air Force	M.E 109F	Messerschmitt 109F (German fighter aircraft)
Div	Division	Savoia Marchetti	Italian – Bomber, Reconnaissance, Transporter

OPERATION 'HUSKY' – the Sicilian Campaign 1943

Contents

- Acknowledgements and Copyright 1
- Key Abbreviations 3
- Introduction 6
  - Background to the formation of the R.A.F. Regiment 6
  - Background to the Mediterranean campaign and Operation 'Husky' 6
  - Operation overview and the role of the R.A.F. Regiment 8
    - Field Squadron – Role and Structure 9
    - Light Anti-Aircraft Squadron – Role and Structure 10
- Pre- Operation 'Husky' deployments - JUNE to JULY 1943 12
  - Overview 12
  - Operational Diaries 15
    - 14th – 30th June 15
    - 1st – 15th July 20
    - 16th – 31st July 23
    - No.2864 LAA Sqn – Map of Flight positions Lampedusa 27
    - No.2864 LAA Sqn - Map detailing the gun positions Lampedusa 28
    - No.2864 LAA Sqn – Account of Activities 29
    - No.2864 LAA Sqn - Movement Order to SOUSSE 31
- Assault Phase - JULY 1943 32
  - Overview 32
  - Operational Diaries 34
    - 14th – 30th June 34
    - 1st – 15th July 35
    - 16th – 31st July 40
    - No.2855 Sqn Ground Defence Operational Order - Lentini West 44
- Follow Up Phase - JULY 1943 46
  - Background 46
  - Operational Diaries 48
    - 1st – 15th July 48
    - 16th – 31st July 50

- No.2904 Sqn. Movement Order 62
- No.2904 Field Squadron Establishment 65

"A" Wing - AUGUST 1943 67

Overview 67

Operational Diaries 69

- 1st – 15th August 69
- 16th – 31st August 77
- No.2855 Sqn - 'Special Flight' Report 86
- No.2855 Sqn Action Report - 11th August 1943 88

"B" Wing - AUGUST 1943 89

Overview 89

Operational Diaries 91

- 1st – 15th August 91
- 16th – 31st August 105
- No.2859 Sqn Operational Orders – San Francesco Landing Ground 114
- No.2859 Sqn Map of Gun Positions – San Francesco Landing Ground 116
- No.2859 Sqn Standing Order for Special A.A. Course 117
- No.2859 Sqn Special A.A. Course – timetable 119

About the Author 120

Other books by the Author 120

Planned books for this operation and campaign series 120

Bibliography 121

Introduction

Background to the formation of the R.A.F. Regiment

Germany's use of airborne troops in Crete, to attack and destroy airfields behind the frontline in May 1941, was a significant change in strategy and Britain had to urgently rethink how it planned the defence of its aerodromes. A Committee was set up in June 1941, chaired by Sir Findlater Stewart, tasked with looking at ways to improve aerodrome defence.

In December 1941, the Cabinet approved a recommendation that the Royal Air Force should form its own aerodrome defence corps. The R.A.F Regiment was formed by Royal Warrant on 6th January 1942 and became operational on 1st February of that year. It wasn't long though, before this newly formed corps would be tested on its first major campaigns in North Africa and the Mediterranean.

Background to the Mediterranean campaign and Operation 'Husky'

Early 1943 was a disaster for the Italy, they lost around 85,000 troops in Russia, and the defeat in the North African campaign, was a combined hammer blow that would weaken the Axis forces for good. The victory in Tunisia opened up the possibility for taking the Italian mainland and Churchill was convinced that following this success, a victory on the Italian mainland would take Italy out of the war. The Mediterranean campaign would start with Operation 'Corkscrew', taking out the fortified islands threatening the Allies advance, followed by Operation 'Husky', the invasion of Sicily and conclude with the taking of the Italian mainland.

Planning for this operation began before the Tunisian victory, and a decision to invade Sicily, rather than Sardinia, originally the more attractive option, took place at the Casablanca conference in January 1943. The Allies greatest treat was posed by the Axis airpower, which effectively disrupted previous combined operations and intelligence estimated that any Sicilian landing would face attacks from just under 800 Axis aircraft. In preparation for Operation 'Husky' the Allies started their air attacks, in May 1943, mainly against airbases in Sicily and Sardinia, however, Greece was also hit to help keep the true target hidden. The focused bombing on the main Sicilian airbases started on 2nd July and by the second week of July, with most of the main airbases either severely damaged or abandoned, the Luftwaffe was forced to move its bomber and fighter bomber groups out of Sicily.

Operation 'Husky' was the codename for the Anglo – American invasion of Sicily, which started on the 9th July 1943, spearheaded by an airborne assault and followed the next day by a combined services seaborne operation. Sicily would fall before the end of August 1943 and Italy's role in this war sealed.

OPERATION 'HUSKY' – the Sicilian Campaign 1943

Map showing the strategic thrust of the Mediterranean campaign

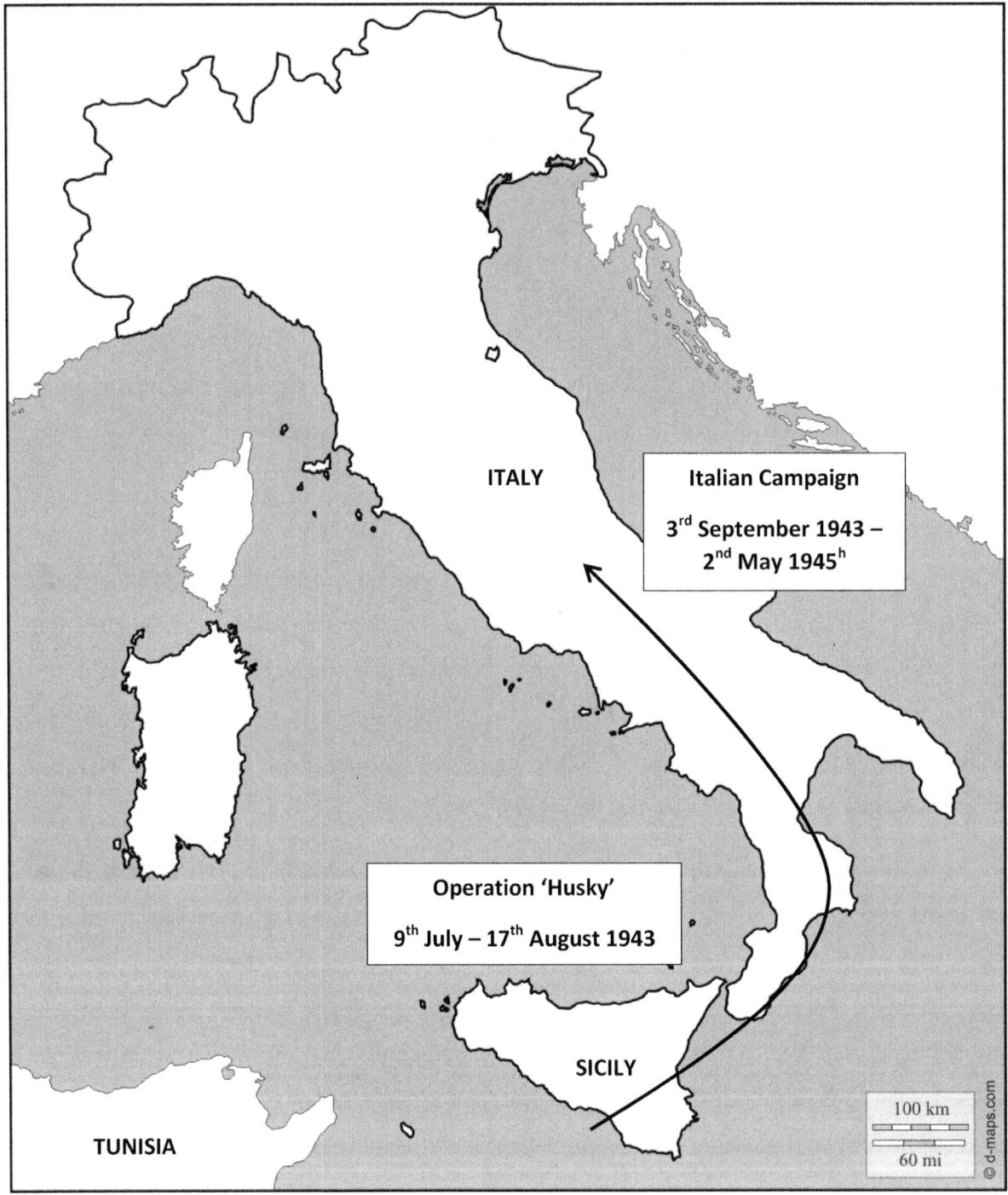

(Source: Author Adapted http://d-maps.com/m/europa/italia/italie/italie03.gif)

OPERATION 'HUSKY' – the Sicilian Campaign 1943

Operation overview and the role of the R.A.F. Regiment

The taking of the west side of the Sicily was the responsibility of the Seventh United States Army, under Lieutenant General Pattern, the east side, was the responsibility of the British Eight Army, which included Canadian forces, under General Montgomery.

It would take just over a month before the Allied forces would receive the Italian surrender, which Lieutenant General Pattern took in Messina on the 17th August 1943.

The Regiment, under the command of Wing Commander Gould, committed 2 Light Anti-Aircraft squadrons to the Assault Phase of the operation, landing near Pachino on the morning of 10th July. To increase the command and control of the squadrons, "informal" Wings were organised for the main phase of the operation, with each Wing, initially commanding 4 squadrons.

The follow up phase of the operation saw four L.A.A. squadrons, from the U.K. land at the port of Augusta on the 19th July and two field squadrons from Egypt, land at the port of Syracuse on the 24th July. By the end of this month, a total of 8 squadrons where in Sicily with just under 1,400 officers and men, protecting advanced landing grounds in the Lentini area.

Map showing the outline of Operation 'Husky' 1943

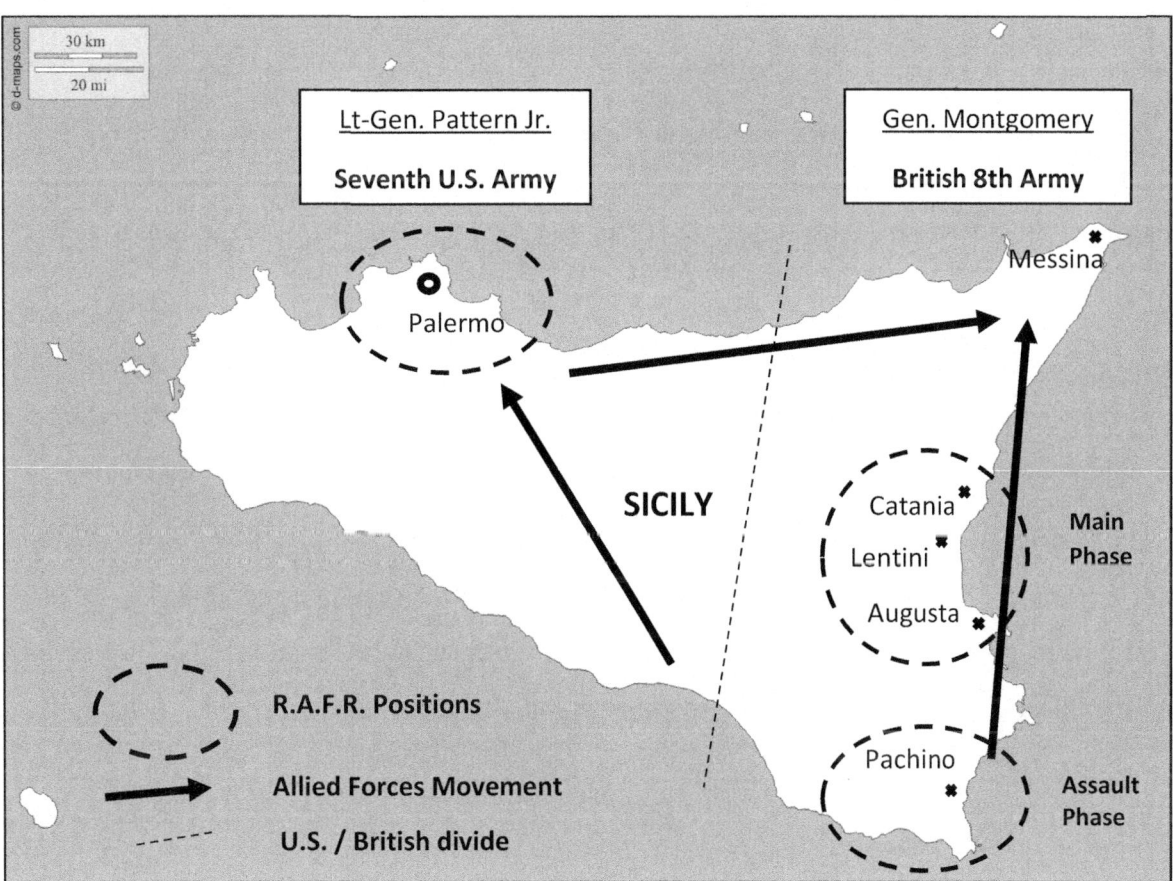

(Source: Author Adapted http://d-maps.com/m/europa/italia/sicile/sicile15.gif)

In August, a further two L.A.A. squadrons arrived on the island, bringing the total number of Regiment squadrons to ten (8 L.A.A. and 2 Field), with an establishment of just over 1,700 officers and men. All, but one of the squadrons were operational around the Lentini - Catania area, a single L.A.A. squadron protected the main aerodrome at Palermo, in the U.S. sector. The Regiments operational effectiveness, however, was hampered by reduced numbers of vehicles and equipment, outbreaks of malaria and restrictions ordered on the Hispano 20 m.m. cannons, due to the danger its non-destructive ammunition, in what was a very crowded area.

Table showing the squadrons on campaign

	'A' Wing		'B' Wing	
Date of arrival	L.A.A. Sqn.	Field Sqn.	L.A.A. Sqn.	Field Sqn.
10th July	2855		2925	
19th July	2858		2856, 2857, 2859	
24th July		2904, 2906		
8th August			2862	
15th August			2864	
TOTAL	2	2	6	Nil

On the 11th August, the enemy aircraft raided the landing grounds in and around Lentini, with devastating effect on the Regiment. Most of the casualties in this operation, killed and injured, happened on this single night, yet it was also a night that saw extreme bravery from the airmen of the R.A.F.R. squadrons.

Field Squadron – Role and Structure
The primary role of the field squadron is to provide ground defence for aerodromes, which included a counter attack capability and an ability to secure, and take control of enemy held aerodromes.

The standard field squadron was organised into six flights, three rifle, one armoured car (sometimes called recce or A.F.V. flights), one support weapons and one headquarters flight. In this operation, the armoured car flights were issued with Morris Light Reconnaissance Cars (LRCs), instead of Humber (LRCs), which became standard for other field squadrons.

Field Squadron establishment (2904 & 2906 ME)

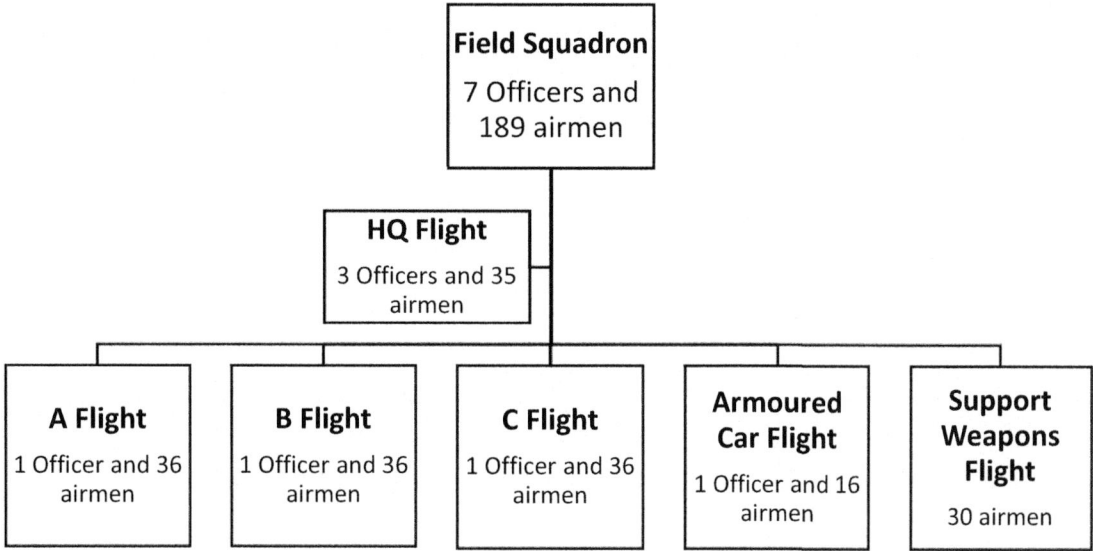

Note: A – C Flights are Rifle Flights.

Light Anti-Aircraft Squadron – Role and Structure

The primary role of the Anti-Aircraft (A.A.) squadron is to provide light anti-aircraft defence, against low-level attacking and dive bombing aircraft. The unit could also use its weapons, if required, in a ground to ground role against tanks and personnel.

The standard L.A.A. squadron had three anti-aircraft flights and one headquarters flight. The squadrons anti-aircraft weaponry evolved between 1942 and 1944, starting with the twin mounted 0.303 Browning machine guns, which were replaced by the 20 m.m. Hispano cannons, which themselves were replaced by the much needed, 40 m.m. Bofor guns. At this stage of the operation, most, but not all squadrons, had been issued with the 20 m.m. Hispano cannon.

Each anti-aircraft flight had a headquarters of six men and 2 sections each of 19 men, with 4 cannons. Each gun crew consisted of 3 airmen, a gun layer, who would aim and fire the gun, a loader, who would load the magazine onto the cannon, and a re-supplier, who would supply the loader with the magazines.

Light Anti-Aircraft Squadron establishment (No.2925 M.E.)

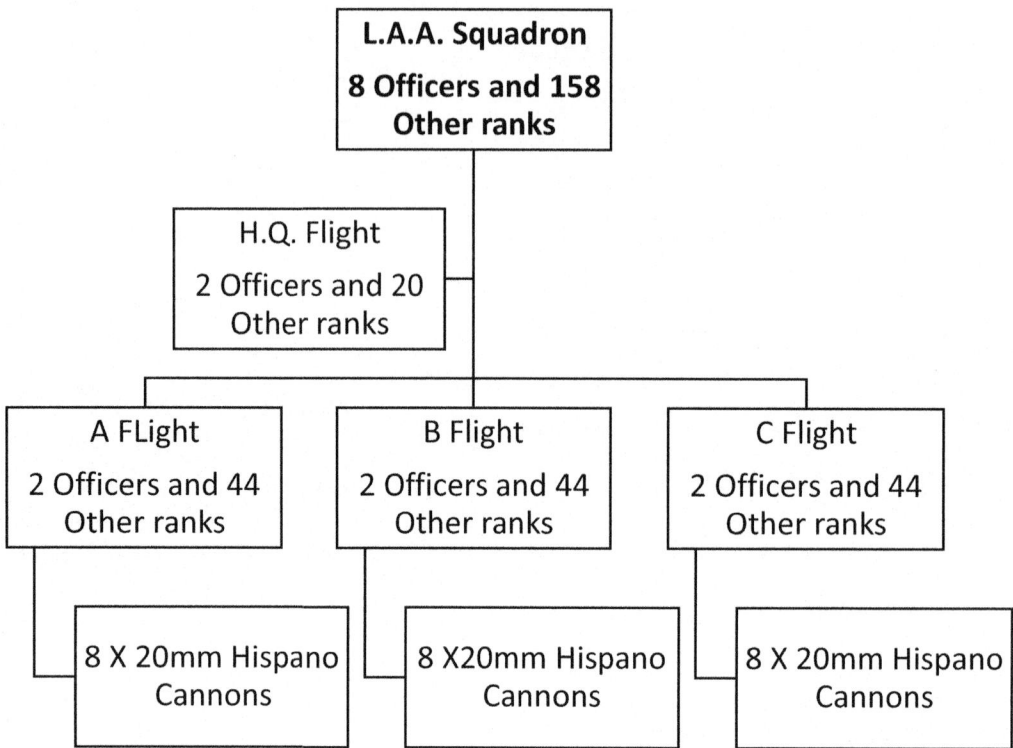

Note: that Flight designations could also be numerical i.e. No.1 to No.3 Flight.

OPERATION 'HUSKY' – the Sicilian Campaign 1943

Pre- Operation 'Husky' deployments - JUNE to JULY 1943

Overview

In preparation for Operation 'Husky', the Allies occupied several Mediterranean islands, in order to maximise the number of land based airfields closer to Sicily. On the 20th June, the defence of the airfield on the island of Lampedusa, mid-way between the Tunisian mainland and Malta, would be the responsibility of 2774 Field and 2864 L.A.A. Squadrons. By the 26th June, 2862 L.A.A. Squadron had landed and occupied the airfield on the island of Gozo, an island touching Malta's northern tip.

In the run-up to for Operation 'Husky', both 2774 and 2864 Squadrons had been categorised as lower priority squadrons and as such, had last call on men, equipment and vehicles. No.2864 L.A.A. Squadron was formed in Grombalia, Tunisia, on the 1st June 1943, combining No. 4341, 4347 and part of 4356 A.A. Flights, with the balance of its establishment coming from 2865 L.A.A. Squadron. It's formal establishment of 6 Officers and 149 O.R.'s, was slightly less than most other related squadrons and its anti-aircraft weaponry consisted, at least on paper, of 28 twin 0.303 Browning machine guns. The squadron's three A.A. Flights (No.1 – No.3), were each allocated 8 twin guns and the remaining 4 twin guns held with the H.Q. flight.

In contrast to this, 2744 Field Squadron was formed at Dyce, Scotland in 1942. As a lower priority squadron for Operation 'Husky', the Support and Armoured Car flights had to hand over their 3" mortars and A.F.V.s to higher priority units. Although the squadron had handed over a significant part of its weaponry and vehicles, although it would have limitations on its role beyond that of a rifle squadron, it retained its 5-flight structure.

On the 18th June 1943, both squadrons, having surrendered any further "surplus" vehicles and equipment for Operation 'Husky', started their embarkation to Lampedusa, on board tank (T.L.C) and infantry (L.C.I.) landing crafts. By the 20th June the main body of the squadrons had landed on the island, with 2744 Squadron taking over the responsibility of the 2nd Battalion Coldstream Guards, for all guards, enemy equipment and material collection, and a significant number of Italian Prisoners of War. The responsibility for the islands Anti-Aircraft defence fell to 2864 Squadron. Following the reconnaissance of the aerodrome, twin mounted 0.303 Browning machine gun posts were positioned, covering the whole of the aerodrome and a large part of the island.

OPERATION 'HUSKY' – the Sicilian Campaign 1943

Map showing the unit positions defending Mediterranean Islands pre- Operation 'Husky'

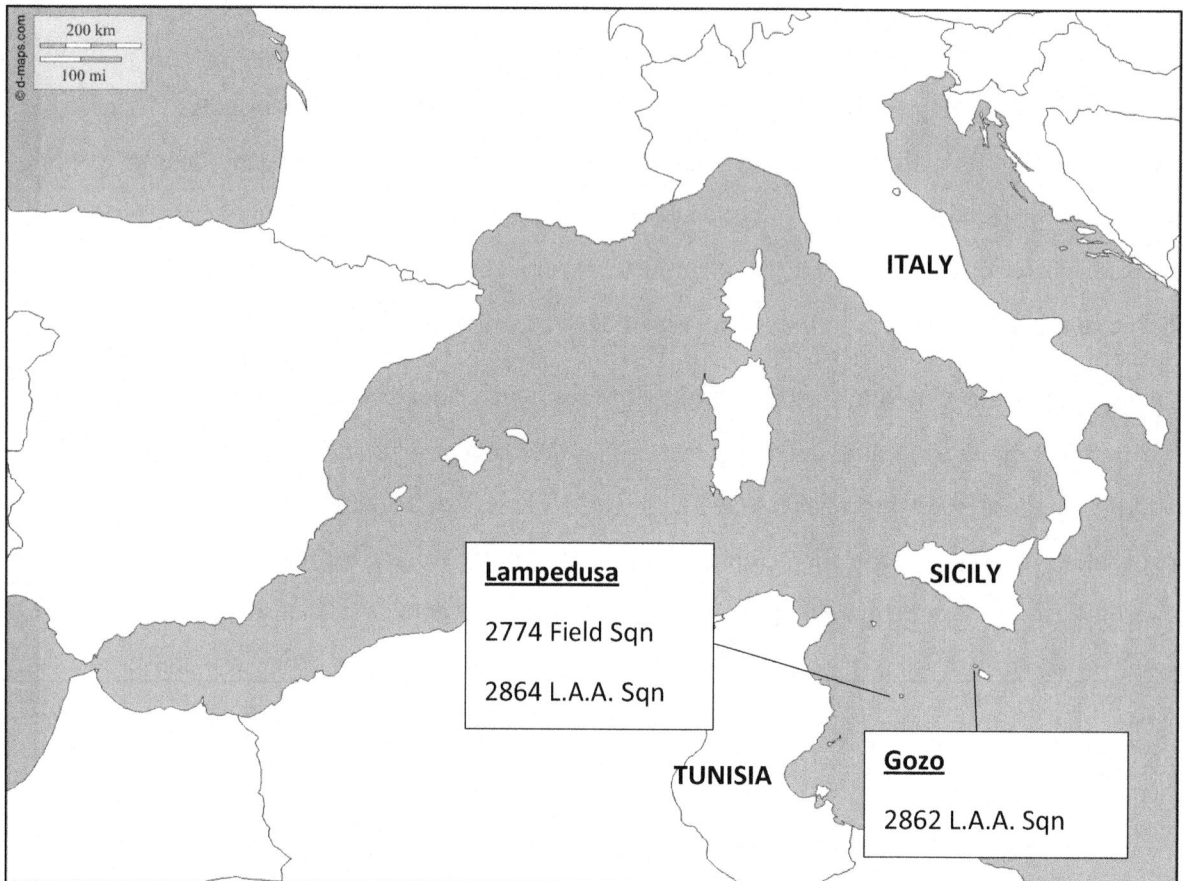

(Source: Author Adapted http://d-maps.com/m/mediterranean/meditoccident/meditoccident05.gif)

The defence scheme for the island and aerodrome officially came into operation at the beginning of July. For 2744 Squadron this included the general routine, guards, patrols, collecting of enemy ammunition, weapons etc., as well as training. Although there were several warnings of approach of potential hostile aircraft, there were no developments for 2864 Squadron to get their teeth into.

On the evening of the 9th July nearly 200 Allied bombers flew over the island, working in conjunction with forces invading Sicily. Although both squadrons were still lacking vital vehicles, most important for the operational duties for 2744 Squadron, several Italian 20m.m. Scotti Isotta Fraschini A.A. Guns had been found, with significant stock of self-destructing ammunition. Although some gun parts were in poor condition and/or damaged, the guns were assembled, tested and fired to a satisfactory level. The Scotti guns were allocated to each flight (No.1 – 2, No.2 – 3 and No.3 – 3) and sited, in conjunction with the 0.303 Browning guns.

The second half of July saw the continuation of general routine for No.2744 Squadron, although with the captured weapons, all personnel had, at least, attained a working knowledge of enemy small arms. Following a successful demonstration, the Air Officer Commanding (A.O.C.) of 242 Group gave 2864 Squadron, the authority to retain all the 20m.m. Scotti guns and ammunition. Soon after which, the squadron received verbal orders to prepare to move to Sousse, Tunisia. On the 30th July, 2864 Squadron left the island and it would be another two months until 2744 Squadron would be able to leave for Tunisia.

Similar to 2864 Squadron, 2862 L.A.A. Squadron was formed in Tunisia, La Marsa, on the 1st June 1943, bringing together 4089, 4340 and half of 4339 A.A. Flights. Its establishment of 8 Officers and 153 O.R.'s, was in line with the standard establishment and the anti-aircraft weaponry included 28 Hispano cannons and 13 0.303 twin Browning Machine Guns. On the 19th June, the squadron embarked from Sousse, Tunisia, stopping very briefly at Valetta, Malta, before proceeding to the aerodrome on the island of Gozo. The squadron positioned and manned its guns, but it soon received orders that the unit's main role would be that of anti-sabotage and anti- parachutist, rather than one of anti-aircraft defence.

The squadron would spend the remainder of it time hauling petrol, bombs, and ammunition between the aerodrome and the docks, as well as general duties and static guards in and around the aerodrome.

OPERATION 'HUSKY' – the Sicilian Campaign 1943

Operational Diaries

14th – 30th June
2744 (Field) Sqn – Embarked from Sousse, Tunisia disembarkation to the island of Lampedusa

S/Ldr. Grace ordered to proceed to SCOUSSE to contact RAF Embarkation Officer reference "GUITAR" force proceeding to LAMPEDUSA. 2744 Squadron with 2864 L/AA Squadron (S/Ldr. Langham) under command, to be assembled at assembly point SOUSSE by 16.00hrs Tuesday 15/6/43. Squadron packed up as far as possible by 20.00hrs.
Reveille 04.30hrs. Squadron packed up and convoy left GAMMART 10.30hrs. Arrived and contacted 2864 Squadron at RUMBALA 12.00hrs, arrived at Map Ref: Tunisia 1/200.000 SOUSSE Sheet 9 4964, north of SOUSSE 17.00hrs.
Squadron kit and equipment inspection, training, bathing parade. S/Ldr. Grace met W/Cdr. Bisdee, D.F.C. O.C. LAMPEDUSA, and attended conference of recce party from the island in the R.A.F. Embarkation Office SOUSSE 10.00hrs.
Spare kit moved to SOUSSE docks. Orders received 17.20hrs from W/Cdr Bisdee, D.F.C., to move two flights from 2864 L/AA Sqdn and one rifle flight from 2744 (Field) Sqdn to decks for embarkation tonight. Convoy ready at camp gate at 18.00hrs. Arrived South jetty, SOUSSE 18.30hrs. T.L.C. left SOUSSE 20.00hrs.
Advanced party arrived LAMPEDUSA. Remainder of 2744 and 2864 Squadrons remain at Map Ref: - Tunisia 1/200.000 SOUSSE Sheet 9 4964. Ordered to stand by ready to move in the morning.
Orders to move, less all transport, personnel to be ready to embark at 15.00hrs. F/O. Harris with drivers ordered to ferry men to docks and then remain with transport in camp area until detailed for embarkation. All personnel, 2744 Sqdn - 6 officer and 124 O.Rs, 2864 Sqdn. - 2 Officer and 56 O.Rs embarked in T.L.C. 116 and left SOUSSE 18.45hrs.
T.L.C. 116 arrived LAMPEDUSA 06.00hrs, disembarked 07.00hrs. Met by W/Cdr. Bisdee D.F.C. on quay, and moved to area EAST of town. T.L.C. 455 with stores not arrived, Squadron being on fatigues slept in the open.
S/Ldr. Grace reported to W/Cdr. BISDEE, D.F.C. and taken to see LT. Col. OGLETHORPE Civil Admin, approximately 3,000 prisoners and 1,800

OPERATION 'HUSKY' – the Sicilian Campaign 1943

civil population still on the island. T.L.C. 455 with stores arrived and prisoners were put to work unloading. Stores for 2744, 2864 and 253 Squadrons transported to Squadron areas. Large batch of prisoners left i/c Colds Guards.
2744 (Field) Squadron take over from 2 Bn. Coldm. Guards and S/Ldr. Grace assumes responsibility for all guards and A/A defence, enemy equipment, prisoners and collection of material on the island. General tour with W/Cdr. BISDEE, D.F.C. 2 Bn Coldm. Guards sailed to-night with batch of prisoners approx. 700, leaving civil population 1500 and 400 - 500 prisoners. Guards placed on Civil Food Store, Petrol, Enemy equipment dump and Magazine.
Guard placed on landing jetty, East bay and patrol on West beach. Takeover all prisoners and enemy transport. F/O. Orbell placed i/c. Movement restricted owing to lack of transport.
Parade of all prisoners and transport 08.00hrs. Check-up shows approx. 400 prisoners.
T.L.C. arrived with two squadron "Jeeps" on board, giving first change to recce the island. This was partly done during afternoon, revealing quantities of weapon and ammunition.
Squadron now have all prisoners and enemy transport under control, also guards on magazine, petrol dump, enemy equipment dump, civil food stores and on both harbours. This leaves one flight to patrol through the island. H.Q established just EAST of LAMPEDUSA TOWN.
Squadron parade and march past at 09.00hrs. Only operational sentries being left on duty. Turn out and general appearance good. Men looked very fit.
Routine work. One flight patrolling the island, remainder doing guards on V.R. and prisoners. Movement very slow owing to lack of any transport for the squadron.
Routine.
General routine. One flight training, patrolling and hardening exercises. Junior N.C.Os under instruction. Present Location: LAMPEDUSA. Sqdn. H.Q. S.E. of town. Rear party 1 Officer and 12 O.Rs with transport pool SOUSSE (Wing pool).

OPERATION 'HUSKY' – the Sicilian Campaign 1943

2864 (LAA) Sqn – Embarked from Sousse, Tunisia disembarkation to the island of Lampedusa

O.C. accompanied S/Ldr, Grace, O.C. 2744 (F) Squadron, R.A.F. Regiment to Sousse to make enquires from R.A.F. Embarkation Unit as to details of embarkation. Embarkation Officer reported that date of move was not certain as shipping was not yet available. This Unit and 2744 Squadron were directed to move to a transit camp approx. 12 miles N. of Sousse. Transport surplus to establishment viz:- 1 Blitz Buggy, 115-cwt Chevrolet, 2 enemy Ford Lorries, 1 3-tonner handed over to O.C. "Bigot" Force.
Squadron left Grombalia in convoy with 2744 Squadron.
Arrived R.A.F. transit camp, Hammam Sousse.
Conference with W/Cdr. Bisdee, Officer Commanding Fighter Wing, moving to Lampedusa. Reports were received from a reconnaissance party which had just returned from the Island. Landing facilities negligible. Water satisfactory. Adequate defence posts, pillboxes and defence dug in solid rock were reported.
Verbal orders received from W/Cdr. Bisdee to embark 2 A.A. Flights on a L.C.I. (Landing Craft Infantry) with equipment at 18.00hrs and one flight of 2744 Squadron.
Nos. 1 and 2 Flights embarked with Flight equipment under Command S/Ldr. Langham and F/Lt Hayes. Squadron H.Q. and No. 3 Flight remained at Sousse with Squadron stores and M.T.
No. 1 and 2 Flights disembarked at Lampedusa Harbour. O.C. made preliminary reconnaissance with Wing Commander Bisdee and sited temporary camp site for personnel, East of town of Lampedusa. These two flights undertook unloading of all equipment (including Wing Equipment) and took over feeding and ration arrangements of all R.A.F. personnel landed pending arrival of further personnel and equipment. It is believed that this Squadron is the first Unit of R.A.F. Regiment to set foot on Metropolitan territory of the enemy.
Nos. 1 and 2 Flights engaged on assembly of guns and camp fatigues, Reconnaissance of aerodrome by O.C. Squadron Headquarters and No. 3 Flight embarked at Sousse with remainder of Squadron Equipment, except 4 3-tonners and stores. One Sgt and 3 A.C's left at Hamman Sousse as rear party.

Squadron Headquarters and No. 3 Flight disembarked at Lampedusa and off-loaded Equipment (including Wing Equipment, rations etc).
No:1 Flight under F/O Hayes took up positions and mounted 8 Twin Browning Guns on South of Coastal side of aerodrome (see sketch map attached).
No. 2 Flight under F/O Wright took up positions and mounted 8 twin Browning Guns on North East side of aerodrome.
No occurrence of importance.
No. 3 Flight took up positions and mounted 7 twin Browning Guns at extreme West of aerodrome. Posts sited to give cover to main harbour, as well as to aerodrome.
Squadron headquarters moved to a blockhouse approx. 400 yards to extreme East of aerodrome. Position commands a view of the whole aerodrome and a large part of the Island.
No occurrence of importance on these dates.
1 Corporal and 7 A.C's detached from No; 2 Flight for A.A. duties with 896 A.M.E.S. at extreme West of Island. Armament 2 Twin Browning Guns belonging to 896 A.M.E.S.
No occurrence of importance.

2862 (LAA) Sqn – Embarked from Sousse, Tunisia disembarkation to the island of Gozo

Training and packing continued.
100% check of all vehicles, and work continued on then to ensure.
Nothing of importance to report.
Embarkation Order received from the Embarkation Officer to proceed to Banjo and form up at No.2 Harbour, Sousse, by 14.00hrs to-day. Squadron moved off and arrived at the docks, proceeding to embark at once aboard L.S.T. Craft No.431.
By 18.00hrs all the Squadron, plus 13 3-ton vehicles and 1 Jeep were aboard. Arrangement for meals were made and the convoy moved out to sea at approximately 19.00hrs the same evening. The whole move was favourably commented upon by the Embarkation Staff and the Captain of the ship. Officers and men carried out their orders to the letter.
Arrived Valetta, Malta, at 17.00hrs., having made the journey

without incident.
Disembarkation took place immediately, movements again being carried out without a hitch. The Captain complimented the Squadron on their behaviour throughout the voyage and on the clean state in which the ship was left.
All personnel and vehicles proceeded to No.11 Transit Camp where meals were provided for the Squadron. No baggage was unpacked and all ranks slept in the open.
Movement Order from the Camp Commandant to proceed at 06.45hrs. on June 26th, 1943, No.11 Harbour, to embark on L.C.T. No.586, at 08.00hrs, for Gozo. Guides were to be provided and personnel were to embark on L.C.I., No.128, at No.10 Wharf. The Embarkation Staff did not know we were moving. The embarkation was carried out and the Captain was able to move out 1 hour before schedule.
Guides were supposed to have been provided, but they failed to appear. The entire Squadron moved off at 06.45hrs. under the Commanding Officer and embarked as per instructions received. En route 1 lorry driver jammed his gears and this was eventually left on the docks together with another lorry for which there was no room aboard, and certain personnel.
The voyage was without incident and the L.C.T. and L.C.I. arrived at Gozo at 12.00hrs. After lying off the harbour for three hours we finally unloaded and proceeded to Gozo aerodrome, where gun positions were sited and living quarters fixed.
The squadron settled in, all guns manned and normal duties carried out.
Signal received from A.H.Q. appointing S/Ldr. Sheil Station Commander of R.A.F. Station, Gozo, wef 28/6/43. Signal received from H.Q. Malta warning of further possible paratroop attacks on aerodromes. Guards warned and patrols placed around the airfield. Commanding Officer contacted Lt. Col. King, Officer Commanding Troops at Gozo and after a reconnaissance of the airfield, gun sites were selected. The guns were moved in and made ready the same day.
The Governor-General of Malta, Lord Gort, V.C. and the G.O.C. arrived by sea. The Commanding Officer was presented to both and conducted them on a tour of the inspection of the aerodrome. They

were very much impressed by all they saw. Signal received from Air Headquarters, Malta, which stated that the Squadron is no longer responsible for the A.A. defence of the aerodrome, but will fulfil the role of anti-sabotage and anti-paratroop defence.
Commanding Officer informed W/Cdr. Coote that the primary role of the Squadron was A.A. duties, but as it was the Air Vice-Marshal's wish the other commitments would be carried out. (This is a case in which a Field Squadron could be better employed). The Americans arrived with 32 Bofors and 32 .5 guns. A Battery of 3 inch guns moved in to-day.

1st – 15th July
2744 (Field) Sqn – Operational routine delivery of the Defence Scheme, plus collection of enemy munitions

MAP REFERENCE. 1: 15840 CB 4096W. Lampedusa and Linosa.
Location. Defence scheme put into official operation. H.Q. 738570.   No.2 Flight. 696587.   No.3 Flight. 746573. Nos 4 and 5 Flights. 739569. No.1 Flight. Guards on enemy magazines (733576), enemy Petrol dump (734575), enemy Equipment and weapons (734572), Civil food stores (731570). L/AA Squadron – area of the aerodrome.
General routine, Guard, patrols, training and collecting enemy ammunition, weapons etc.
Routine.
Squadron parade 09.00hrs, inspection, speech and march past Commander C.A.F. Lampedusa (W/Cdr. J.D. Bisdee, D.F.C.).
Routine.
Flight preparing new concentration areas.
Routine.
No. 182 H.S.L. arrived Cala Pisana. Boom closed in main harbour.
Late at night large number of aircraft passed over flying very low.
Attack on Sicily started.
Routine.

OPERATION 'HUSKY' – the Sicilian Campaign 1943

F/Lt. Featonby left by boat for SOUSSE to try and collect equipment etc., to bring squadron up to operational scale
Routine.

2864 (LAA) Sqn – Operational routine at aerodrome, acquisition of Italian 20m.m. A.A. Guns

3 Twin .303 Browning Guns and mountings complete were handed over to this squadron by 253 Fighter Squadron being surplus to their establishment.
Two 3-ton Bedford lorries arrived from Sousse, having been dispatched by means of Tank Landing Craft.
One .303 Twin Browning sent to No.3 Flight (W. of aerodrome) to complete the establishment of 8 twin guns and mounted. MENTIONED IN DISPATCHES. A copy of Command Routine Orders Ser. No.16, dated 9th June, 1943 was received by this Unit today. No.110461 F/Lt. H.S. Gibbs (Ex 4341 A.A. Flight and 614 Squadron) now second in command of this Unit, was recorded as having been Mentioned in Dispatches.
Wing Commander Bisdee D.F.C. inspected Squadron H.Q. and Nos.1 and No.3 Flights.
Warning of hostile aircraft in the vicinity. No further development.
Warning received from Operations of the approach of hostile aircraft.
No developments.
No occurrence of importance.
S/Ldr. Symons, R.A.F. Regiment Staff officer, 242 Group visited this H.Q. Warning of hostile aircraft in the vicinity. No development.
No occurrence of importance.
Large number of aircraft in near vicinity. Information received from Operations that there were 200 friendly bombers slightly North flying W. to E. (operating in conjunction with forces invading Sicily).
No occurrence of importance.
Rear Party arrived from Sousse with remainder of Unit Equipment, including 2 3-ton Bedford lorries and new Spider Mountings for all .303 Twin Brownings held by this Unit.
C.O. attended Unit Commander's Conference held by Wing Commander

OPERATION 'HUSKY' – the Sicilian Campaign 1943

> Bisdee, D.F.C.
>
> Matter under discussion included draft Defence Scheme prepared by S/Ldr. Grace, O.B.E. 2744 Squadron R.A.F. Regiment, military precautions, medical arrangements and general matters of island administration affecting units. Similar conferences to be held weekly.

> The assembly of 9 20m.m. Scotti Isotta Fraschini A.A. Guns was completed by Squadron H.Q. Several of these guns had been recovered in a badly neglected state and others had been damaged by enemy sabotage necessitating parts being recovered from other damaged guns to enable complete assembly.
>
> The guns are complete with carriage from which they can be quickly dismounted and can be towed by light vehicles. Their method of construction renders assembling and dismantling comparatively easy and quick.
>
> Estimated effective range is 2,500 yards. Type of ammunition available are armour piercing and high explosive (self-destroying at approximately 2,500 yards). Estimated stocks in island magazine not less than 160,000 rounds.
>
> Several sets of tools and spare parts acquires.
>
> All guns tested and fired in the presence of Wing Commander Bisdee D.F.C., Military Governor of Lampedusa and Lt. Comdr. Dale Naval Officer i/c. Tests proved satisfactory in each case.

> 3 20m.m. Isotta guns allocated to each Flight (Except No.1 Flight) and sited by O.C. and Second i/c in conjunction with Flight Commanders. 2 guns only allocated to No.1 Flight owing to lack of suitable site, 1 being retained temporarily for mounting at H.Q.

> All 20m.m. Isotta Guns mounted, at sites selected, by each Flight. The disposition of .303 Twin Browning and 20m.m. Isotta Guns is set out in the sketch map annexed.

> 1 further 20m.m. Isotta completely assembled and mounted at H.Q. Total now in use:- 10.

2862 (LAA) Sqn – Operational anti- sabotage /parachute & other duties at aerodrome

> The following is an extract from A.H.Q. (Malta) signal 0.620 dated June 29th, "O.C. 2862 L.A.A. Squadron, R.A.F. Regiment is to be

used primarily for anti-sabotage and anti-parachute duties on the aerodrome and also guarding of aircraft at night but is to co-ordinate defence organisation with Army Command". 3 N.C.O.s and 30 airmen attached to Commandoes for aerodrome duties. Other personnel on Dock work with lorries.
Nothing of importance to report.
Transport used for hauling petrol and bombs etc. from docks to aerodrome.
F/O Bonthron admitted to hospital.
Nothing of importance.
Transport and Gunner employed unloading Barges of Petrol and ammunition.
40 men detached from Commandoes on completion of aerodrome duties.

16th – 31st July
2744 (Field) Sqn – Operational routine delivery of defence scheme and disposal of enemy munitions

Routine.
Lt.Col. Shutti, R.A. and Col. H.S. Lowry, U.S.A. rearmament committee visited the Island to see captured equipment and ammunition.
Routine
Visit by A.O.C. No.242 Group Air Commodore Cross, D.S.O., D.F.C.
F/Lt. Featonby arrived back by T.L.C. from SOUSSE with F/O Middleton and 22 O.Rs posted to squadron.
Routine.
Boat in from SOUSSE.
Routine.
Visit by A.V.M. Sir Hugh Pugh Lloyd, K.B.E., C.B., M.C., D.F.C., from H.Q. N.A.C.A.F.
2864 L/AA Squadron left by boat for SOUSSE.
Three lorry loads of hand grenades and other loose explosives taken out to sea and dumped. During the month nearly all squadron personnel have attained working knowledge of enemy small arms.

OPERATION 'HUSKY' – the Sicilian Campaign 1943

2864 (LAA) Sqn – Operational routine, disembarkation back to Sousse, Tunisia

No occurrence of importance on these dates.
O.C. attended Unit Commanders conference held by Wing Commander Bisdee, D.F.C. Matters of administration, discipline and sports discussed.
No occurrence of importance on these dates.
Air Commodore Cross, A.O.C. 242 Group visited this H.Q. During his visit he inspected a 20m.m. Scotti Issotta Fraschini Gun and requested a demonstration fire practice. He gave authority for the guns held to be retained by this Unit.
A telephone message was received from Wing H.Q. to the effect that a signal had been received from H.Q. 242 Group ordering movement of this Unit to Sousse forthwith to report to 1st A.D.W. (see copy of signal annexed).
Authority given by Wing H.Q. to dismantle all .303 Twin Browning Guns, to take 20m.m. Isotta Guns and as much ammunition as possible.
All .303 Twin Brownings dismantled and equipment packed and crated ready to move.
Section of No.1 Flight detached to 896 A.M.E.S. recalled 2 Officers reported for duty with this Unit namely 108847 F/O J.A. Henson and 123706 F/O F. Winfield.
No occurrence of importance.
This Unit ready awaiting embarkation on first available ship.
Loaded equipment on S.S. Empire Dace. Finally embarked and left Lampedusa at 15.00hrs.
S.S. Empire Dace ran aground on a sandbank. Understood from ship's Captain that ship was 7 miles off course 25 S. of Sousse. Ship's crew spent morning endeavouring to move ship from sandbank.
Ship visited by N.O.I.C. to send Air Sea Rescue Launch. Arrangements made by N.O.I.C. to send 3 L.C.I's to transfer personnel owing to lack of water and 1 L.C.T. to transfer cargo from Empire Dace to lighten load.
O.C. and Second i/c this Unit returned with N.O.I.C. to Sousse to make arrangements for transport to Tunis. F/Lt. Hayes left in Command Squadron and detailed to leave 1 Officer and 3 N.C.O's and 21 men with equipment on Empire Dace if personnel transferred to

OPERATION 'HUSKY' – the Sicilian Campaign 1943

another ship.
O.C. visited Embarkation Officer at Sousse on landing, who stated that he had received instructions that this Unit was not now to proceed and was to be held at Sousse – ultimate destination unknown to him. O.C. telephoned 242 Group for Orders. Orders received that this Unit was to proceed to Tunis as soon as possible and transport was to be arranged by Embarkation Officer, Sousse, either at Sousse or through Transport Officer Tunis. Informed Embarkation Officer, Sousse of these orders.
Main party on Empire Dace under F/Lt. Hayes transferred with personal equipment on to an L.C.I. for disembarkation at Sousse.

2862 (LAA) Sqn – Operational anti-sabotage/parachute & other duties at aerodrome

P/O. Odgers promoted F/O. wef 26/12/42.
F/O. Odgers admitted Victoria Hospital. A.O.C. visited the aerodrome and was conducted round by the C.O. S/Ldr. Sheil.
F/Lt. Jones admitted 90th General Hospital.
Nothing to report.
Inspection of all M.T. Vehicles. Information from Malta that no spare-parts for Bedfords or Thornycrofts available. 3 lorries unserviceable.
Nothing to report.
F/O. Odgers discharged from hospital.
Nothing to report.
Air raid 03.00 – 04.00hrs. Bombs dropped N.W. of island, no casualties. Barrage put up by Army Bofors.
F/O. Bonthron discharged from 90th General Hospital. F/O.s Chanin and Short proceeded to Valetta on Temporary Duty re. Pay Books.
Nothing to report.
F/O.s Chanin and Short returned from Valette.
F/O. Chanin admitted to Victoria Hospital.
Nothing to repot.
Owing to the duties being carried out by the Squadron, the guns

were only partially manned during the month.

No.2864 LAA Sqn – Map of Flight positions Lampedusa

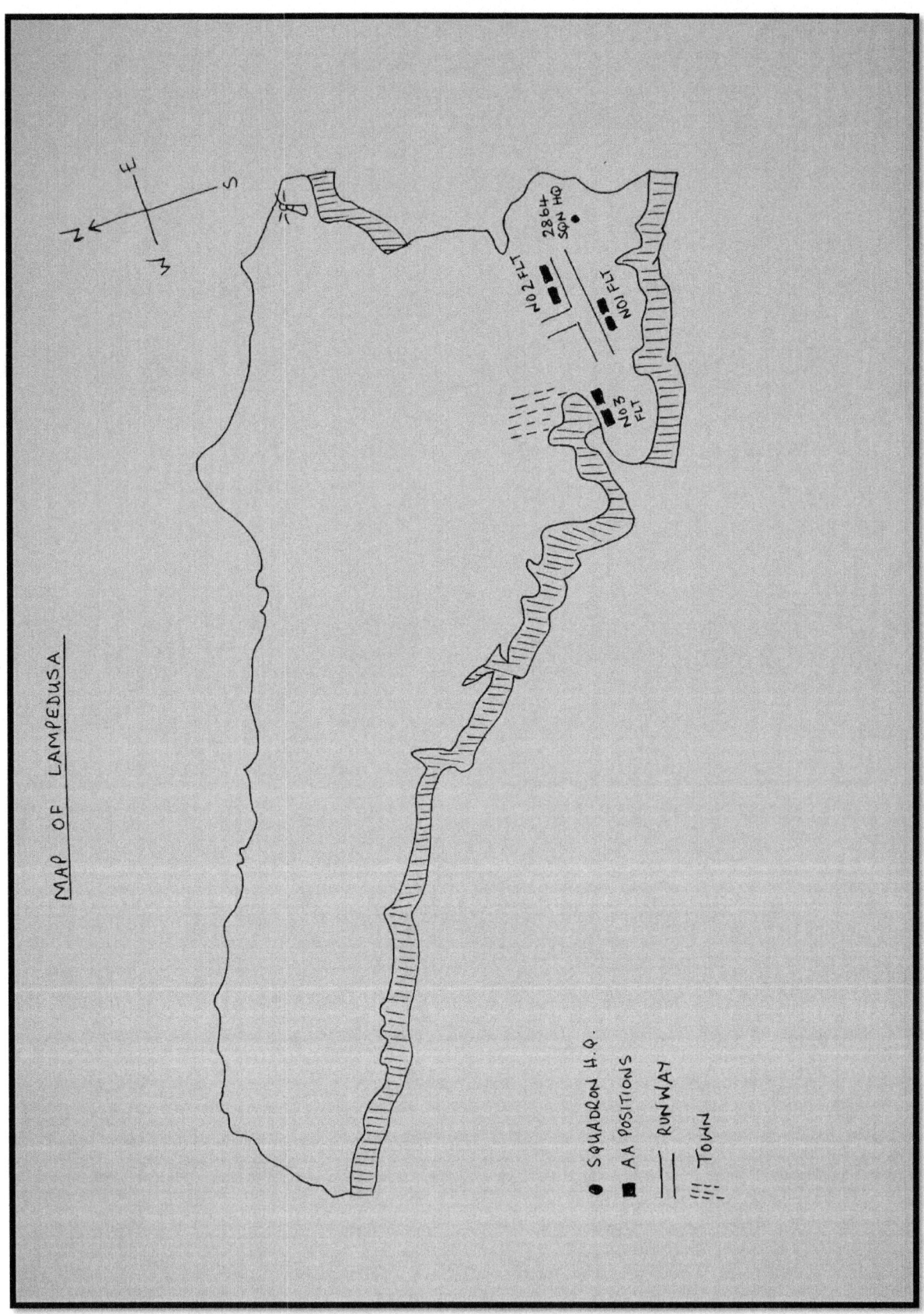

(Author copy of original sketch map)

OPERATION 'HUSKY' – the Sicilian Campaign 1943

No.2864 LAA Sqn - Map detailing the gun positions Lampedusa

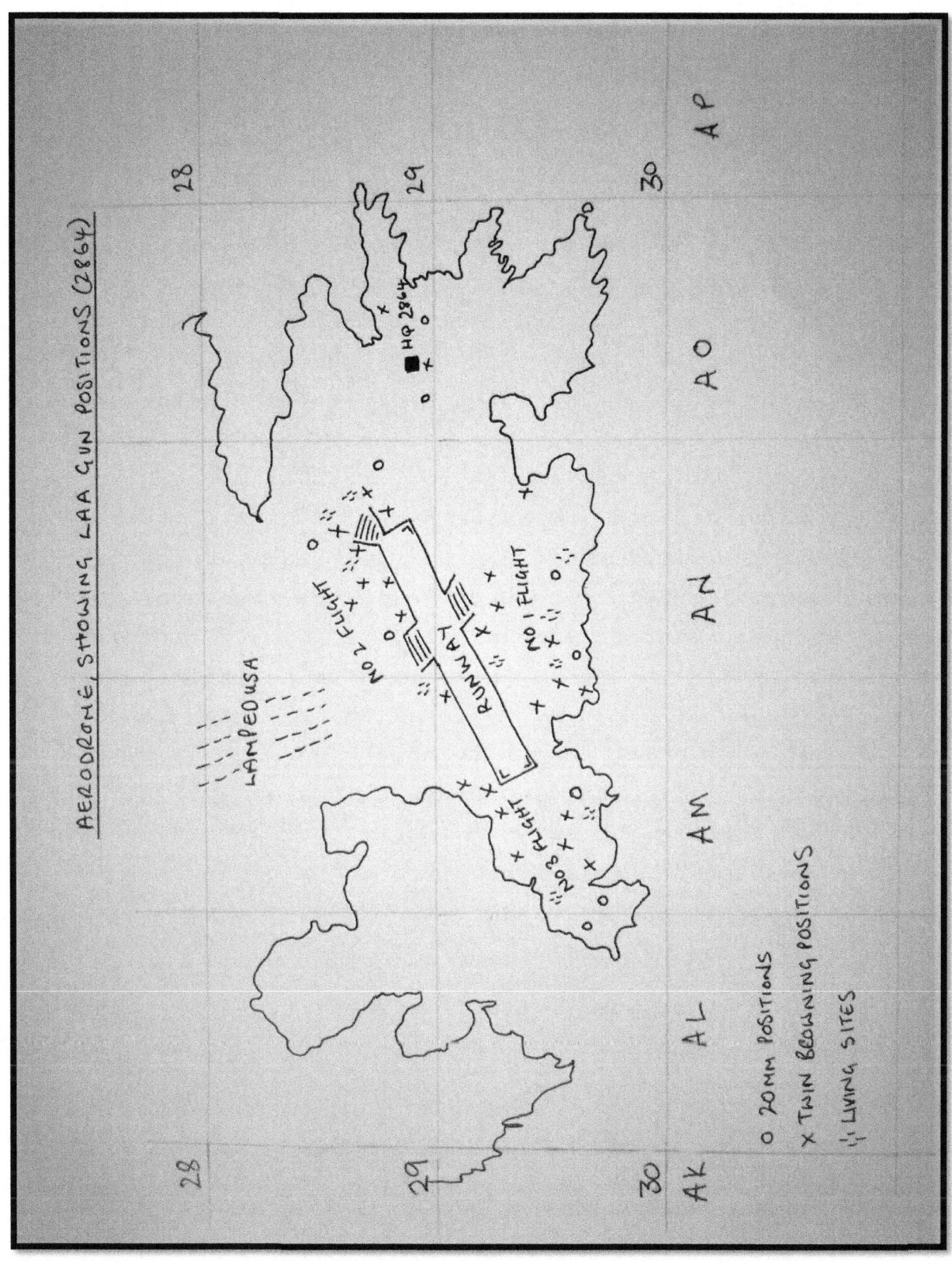

(Author copy of original sketch map)

No.2864 LAA Sqn – Account of Activities

APPENDIX   I.

Account of Activities of:-

1352934   Sgt. Arthur Stuart Cheetham.

At approximately 11.05 hours on 30.6.43 at C.A.F. Lampedusa a Boston aircraft overran the runway and crashed into a pile of debris some 150 yards beyond on the vicinity of the Flight H.Q. of No.3 Flight 2864 L.A.A. Squadron. No. 1352934 Sgt. Cheetham A.S. the N.C.O. i/c ran to the scene of the crash and arrived as one member of the crew making exit from the rear upper gun turret. Another member of the crew was badly trapped under the damaged nose of the machine and the pilot was trapped by one foot. There were already several small fires burning in the lower part of the cockpit and a considerable quantity of .303 ammunition was exploding inside the cockpit owing to the heat of the fire. Sgt. Cheetam immediately detailed an airman to call the ambulance and fire tender by telephone and organised all airmen in the vicinity to bring all water available to help extinguish the flames. He himself took an active part in hacking holes in the aircraft, in the face of fire and exploding ammunition, which resulted in the trapped members of the crew being extricated.

As a result of his immediate action the fire was kept under control until the arrival of the fire tender and the life of one member of the crew was ultimately saved.

OPERATION 'HUSKY' – the Sicilian Campaign 1943

Account of the Activities of:-

<u>1470164   Cpl. Frank Edward Wepener</u>

At approximately 11.05 hours on 30.6.43 at C.A.F. Lampedusa a Boston aircraft overran the runway and crashed into a pile of debris some 150 yards beyond on the vicinity of the Flight H.Q. of No.3 Flight 2864 L.A.A. Squadron. One member of the crew was badly trapped under the damaged nose of the machine and the pilot was trapped by one foot. Several small fires immediately started in the lower part of the cockpit and a considerable quantity of .303 ammunition was exploding inside the cockpit owing to the heat of the fire. No. 1470164 Corporal Wepener who was in the vicinity exercised presence of mind by immediately obtaining an axe, and in the face of the fire and exploding ammunition hacked holes in the side of the machine which resulted in the trapped members of the crew being extradited, and enabled water to reach the fire and eventually extinguish it. By his determined efforts the fire was prevented from spreading and the life of one member of the crew was ultimately saved.

No.2864 LAA Sqn - Movement Order to SOUSSE

<u>COPY</u>.

Sub Form 96

<u>MESSAGE FORM.</u>

TO: C.A.F. Lampedusa   Sousse Sector   RRR NACAF NAAF Adv.

From. H.Q. 242 Group   0.435   24/7   MOST SECRET.

2864 A.A. SQUADRON AND 896 A.M.E.S. TO MOVE TO SOUSSE FORTHWITH TO REPORT TO 1ST. A.D.W. (.) SIGNAL EFFECTIVE DATES NUMBER OF PERSSONNEL AND VEHCILES BY TYPES (.) NO REPLACEMENST REPEAT REPLACEMENTS UNITS WILL PROCEED LAMPEDUSA (.)

Deciphered by

Sgt. Lambert.   IMMEDIATE   TOO 241615B.

Assault Phase - JULY 1943

Overview

The first two Regiment squadrons ashore in the assault phase, on the 10th July, were 2855 (LAA) from the U.K. and 2925 (LAA) from Egypt. Leaving the U.K. in mid-June, 2855 Squadron had an uneventful voyage until they were off the coast of Algeria, near Oran, where the convoy was attacked by U boats. One of the ships carrying the squadrons vehicles and equipment was sunk, with the loss of 8 Hispano cannons, and several 3-ton Bedford's, jeeps and motorcycles.

With landing points ploughed or blocked , the morning landing on the beaches for 2855 Squadron were not without incident, with some sections having to swim ashore, in full kit. As Pachino airfield was still occupied by the enemy, the squadron had to wait for some time in its designated assembly area. With a limited number of available vehicles the squadron made its way independently to the airfield, siting its remaining 4 Hispano guns protecting the N-S runway. The shipping and beaches continued to be attacked by enemy aircraft and although no direct attacks were aimed on the airfield, as soon as the aircraft came in range, the guns would engage.

Map showing the 'Assault' Phase of Operation 'Husky' – July 1943

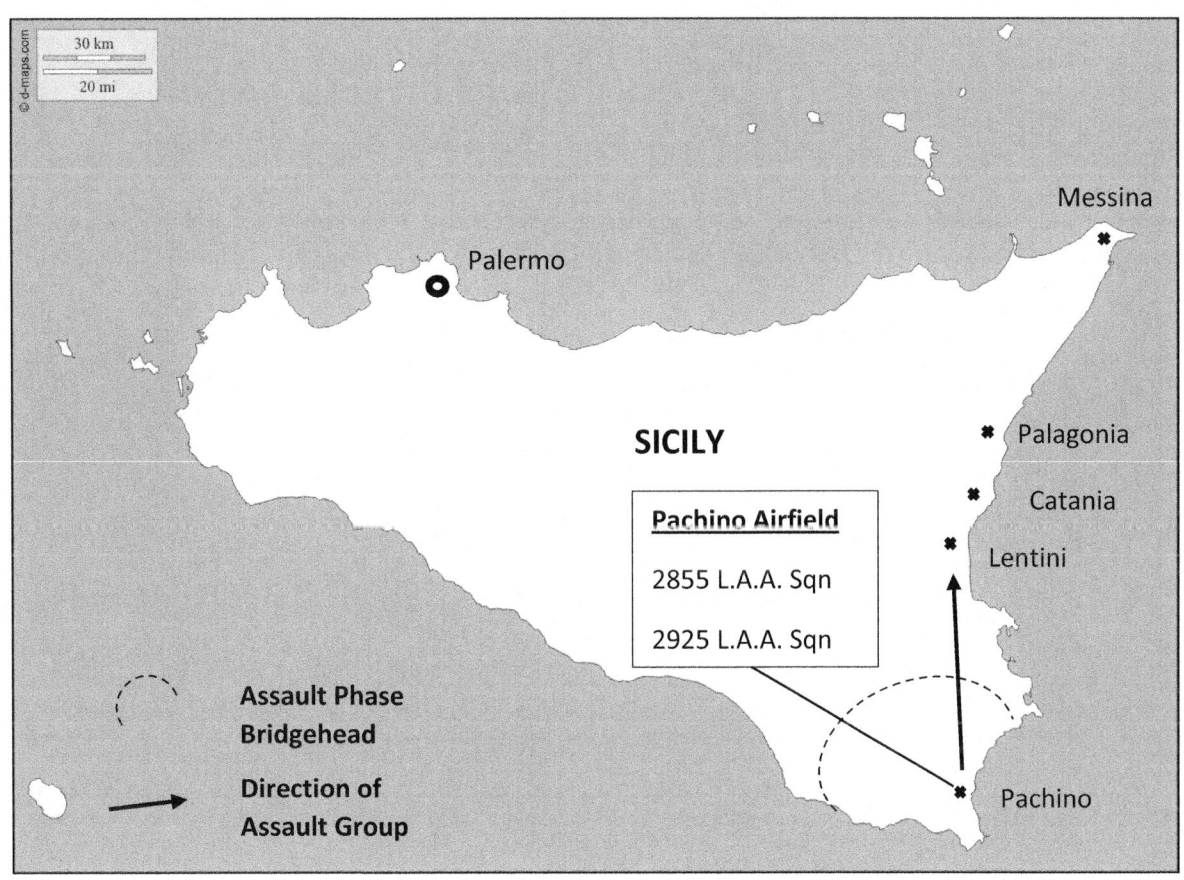

(Source: Author Adapted http://d-maps.com/m/europa/italia/sicile/sicile15.gif)

OPERATION 'HUSKY' – the Sicilian Campaign 1943

Early in July 2925 Squadron set out from Port Said, Egypt and soon learnt that their destination was to be Sicily, morale was high, with the general feeling of "Look out Musso, here we come". The voyage and landing on the beaches was without major incident and with most of its vehicles, the squadron proceeded to Pachino airfield. There was great banter between the squadrons on their first meet, with 2925 Squadron finding the UK squadrons, combination of berets and white knees strikingly different to that of the seasoned campaigners of the Middle East. Although the last laugh was on 2925 squadron, when in their first action all guns went u/s, after a few rounds, due to faulty firing cables.

In the last half of the month both squadrons were ordered to move to the Lentini landing grounds, with 2864 Squadron initially responsible for the Lentini West and 2925 Squadron the Lentini East runways. A rifle flight was formed by members of 2864 Squadron for a Special Mission to move into Catania as soon as it fell, its role to secure requisitioned assets.

OPERATION 'HUSKY' – the Sicilian Campaign 1943

Operational Diaries

14th – 30th June
2855 (LAA) Sqn – At Sea en-route from the United Kingdom to Sicily

Squadron arrived at GREENOCK.
Squadron in two parties, embarked in their respective transports: No.1 party under S/Ldr. Kinchett 78 personnel in S.S. Circassia. No.2 party under F/Lt. T.J. Tarry 59 personnel in S.S. Langibby Castle. The Squadron M.T. was divided between three ships: B.B.2 B.B.3 and B.B.4 F/O. E. Mansfield was Officer i/c Transport on Ship B.B.4 During the voyage personnel aboard "CAIRCASSIA" manned the Oerlikon A.A. Guns and those on board "LANGIBBY CASTLE" maintained anti-U boat watch. All of the above ships sailed in convoy "HERRICK I". Two exercises were carried out on the coast of AYR before the convoy sailed.
M.T. Convoy sailed from GREENOCK.
Troopship convoy sailed from GREENOCK. Troopship convoy encountered submarine activity in Mediterranean. Escort vessels destroyed one U boat. No enemy aircraft sighted. Casualties and sickness – Nil. M.T. Convoy attacked by U boats in Mediterranean off ORAN. Ships B.B.3. was torpedoed and sunk (Date not available) Vehicles on this ship were: Four 3 ton Bedfords packed to capacity with Squadron equipment including 8 Hispano A.A. Guns complete with magazines and ammunition, Two Jeeps and Four Motor Cycles. No information regarding the six airmen of this Squadron on board the vessel is yet available.

OPERATION 'HUSKY' – the Sicilian Campaign 1943

1st – 15th July
2855 (LAA) Sqn – Sea borne Assault group disembarkation at Pachino – Operational at Pachino Airfield

Message received on board S.S. "CIRCASSIA" from W/Cdr. Abrahams (S.S. "HILLARY") informing me of loss of B.B.3. Information regarding personnel still not available.
METEOR. Weather fine. Cloudless. Visibility good. Sea calm.
Squadron stood to on Mess Deck of CIRCASSIA to disembark in assault craft.
Party on CIRCASSIA embarked on L.C.I. (L) for "Sugar Green Beach, Bark South" L.C.I. (L) unable to clear sandbanks obstructing beach and was forced to beach in eight feet of water. With aid of land line, however, party swam ashore in full kit. Casualties – NIL. Equipment lost – 1 Bren Gun, 1 Revolver. Party proceeded to Assembly are "BEAVER" and were met by F/Lt. Tarry, who had just arrived with his party.
F/Lt. Tarry's Report on Landing of his Party. Troops disembarked from "LANGIBBY CASTLE" in two L.C.I.s.
No.1 Party (F/O. J. Lindop i/c) landed on beach without incident at 08.00hrs.
No.2 Party (F/Lt. Tarry i/c) was delayed by mine clearing operations and landed at 08.30hrs.
Party proceeded to assembly area and the whole squadron linked up at 09.30hrs.
Airfield still in enemy hands. Information scarce and confused. Squadron carried out the following drill in assembly area: Removed mae west. Cleaned weapons. Rested.
I endeavoured to contact C.R.E. in "Bitch" assembly area as ordered, but was unable to make contact. I proceeded to airfield to ascertain position and was instructed by Lt/Col. Dennison C.R.E. to move Squadron up on a.m. D + 1. (Airfield had been ploughed up by enemy prior to evacuation)
Heavy bombing by enemy aircraft directed at convoy anchored of "BARKWEST"
METEOR. Weather fine. No cloud. Visibility good. I proceed to airfield to carry out a reconnaissance in conjunction

OPERATION 'HUSKY' – the Sicilian Campaign 1943

with C.R.E. and A.A.D.C. Instructions were issued to 2nd i/c to move up Squadron to R.V. West side of airfield at 09.00hrs.

Recce. Completed. Area East and West of N.-S. runway given to me as Squadron area. Met Squadron at R.V. F/Lt. Farnworth had brought Squadron up with the following information: Vehicles not yet available but 2nd i/c had proceeded to beach to ascertain position. Flights moved off to selected areas independently.

2nd i/c reported to Squadron H.Q. with 2 three ton Bedfords and two Jeeps. Information regarding balance of M.T. very obscure, owing to difficulties of beaching. Many beaches were false and workable one churned up. He had, however, arranged with the Officer i/c Beaver Assembly Are M.T. for the redirecting of Squadron transport to the airfield.

We had at this stage four A.A. guns only. These allocated to No.1 Flight, and immediately placed in position.

S.S. "CIRCASSIA" moved off without unloading Officers' kits. Three Officers' kits were therefore not available.

Airfield attacked by 5 M.E. 109Fs approaching out of the sun at 50 feet and less. Guns took action without success.
Ammunition expenditure: 32 rounds 20m.m.

Information received that enemy snipers were still in the area.

METEOR. Weather fine. No cloud. Visibility good.

Shipping and beaches again bombed by enemy aircraft, but on smaller scale than previous night. Aircraft out of range of our guns. No action taken.

Co-ordinated with units on flanks a system of night sentry watches.

Attended conference of all A.A. Unit Commanders at Corps H.Q. General scheme of positions, barrage and communications discussed. Major Harris (Temporary A.A.D.C.) suggested scheme of communication for this squadron – telephone line from nearest 208 set to Squadron H.Q. The 208 set received information from G.O.R. Information from Squadron H.Q. passed by 18 set to three 38 sets per flight. Telephones at this stage unobtainable.
No. 2925 Squadron (ex M.E.) allocated to N – S runway.
No. 2855 Squadron allocated to North side of E.- W. runway.

Squadron moved to new area. Recce. of 3 flight area completed. All guns in position and manned by 18.00hrs.

OPERATION 'HUSKY' – the Sicilian Campaign 1943

RATIONS. Arranged for flights to eat on their own sites as compo rations would be issued for the next 21 days. WATER. Abundant supply of drinking water available in this area.
Shipping on beaches again attacked, enemy aircraft flying directly over airfield. Barrage put up from airfield most satisfactory. A.A. Guns at this period defending airfield numbered over 100. Ammunition expenditure: 313 rounds 20m.m.
METEOR. Weather fine. No cloud. Visibility good.
Airfield ready to receive aircraft.
Attended conference of all A.A. Unit Commanders at G.O.R. Those present included Lt/Col. Matthews 75th Battery A.A.D.O. Pachino Airfield. General discussion on arrival of new A.A. Units. Dispositions arranged. A.A.D.C. suggested sending 1 A.A. Squadron R.A.F. Regiment to assist in defence of new A.L.G. when ready.
Visited at Squadron H.Q. by Station Commander. Vehicles required by No. 244 Wing to remove equipment from beaches. Co-operated by lending four 3 ton Bedfords.
Enemy aircraft attacked convoy off beaches. Barrage from airfield most effective. One E.A. shot down near airfield. Two of the flights claimed hits and assisted in the destruction of the aircraft. Duration of raid 50 minutes. MEDICAL. On the instruction of the S.M.O. No. 244 Airfield No. 1694731 A.C.2 Spiby J. was graded unfit and returned to U.K. Ammunition expenditure: 1069 rounds 20m.m.
METEOR. Weather fine. No cloud. Visibility good.
Contacted W/Cdr. Hackett No.4 Beach Group who informed me that personal kit on ship E.E.14 had now arrived and would be delivered direct to PACHINO Airfield. Spitfire squadrons arrived from Malta. Supplies of 20m.m ammunition and petrol now available.
Empire News intercepted on 18 sets. Copies typed and distributed to flights. This will now be a daily distribution. No action during the night.
METEOR. Weather fine. No cloud. Visibility good.
Water supplies supplemented with local stocks of wine. Order issued to dilute wine with water.
Arrival of Lt/Col. C.D. Bowdery M.C. and F/Lt. Whitbread R.A.F.

OPERATION 'HUSKY' – the Sicilian Campaign 1943

Regiment.
S/Ldr. Disney S.L.A. No. 244 Wing visited Squadron H.Q.
Squadron concert organised for men off duty.
Short sharp raid on shipping. Raiders engaged without success. Ammunition expenditure 1094 rounds 20m.m.

2925 (LAA) Sqn – At Sea from Egypt, Sea borne Assault group disembarkation at Merzemimi – Operational at Pachino Airfield

All Units from all vessels taking part in operation "BIGOT HUSKY YO", anchored at PORT SAID, landed in the morning in three batches and marched through the town an along the esplanade to a point on the beach about three miles west of the town to exercise the men, give them a chance to get thoroughly clean and to relieve the monotony of troopship life.
All vessels sailed from PORT SAID.
Instructions were issued that sealed orders were to be opened and troops learned that the operation was to be the invasion of SICILY. The announcement was met with no surprise but all troops began to speculate whether the operation was in reality a feint designed to cover a larger attack elsewhere after continuous repetition in the newspapers of the strength of the enemy in SICILY. News broadcasts were followed very closely, especially reports on Allied air attacks on Sicilian airfields. The whole plan of campaign was explained to all personnel during the voyage with the assistance of models, aerial photographs and handbooks and by the time we were nearing the Sicilian coast, all personnel knew exactly what his particular role was to be, where to go on landing and were familiar enough with landmarks in the vicinity of the landing beaches to enable them to link up with Units if for any reason they were split up. The moral of all troops was extremely good and few, if any, would have missed the show. The general feeling was "Look out Musso, here we come". And all ranks of the R.A.F. were confident of the result on being told we were operating with the Eight Army.

OPERATION 'HUSKY' – the Sicilian Campaign 1943

Convoy arrived in the vicinity of MALTA without incident. During the day a large convoy of merchant ships and L.C.T's was passed.
Invasion force arrived off S.E. coast of SICILY. Assault force consisting of Hampshires, Dorsets and Devons and went ashore at MERZEMIMI and landed without much opposition.
Unit embarked in L.C.A's and proceeded to beaches, landing without mishap and proceeded to assembly area of Airfields Group. The 48 hour rations were sampled and voted very good; the inclusion of sweet biscuits among the "hard tack" was especially welcomed. During the day only one enemy aircraft was seen but about 22.00hrs enemy aircraft attacked the beaches and transports. The attack was driven off before any damage had been done by the A/A barrage.
Enemy aircraft again attacked beaches and transports in the early morning, one stick of bombs dropping very near Airfields Group assembly area.
Unit moved to PACHINO airfield and sites recce'd for gun posts and Flight H.Q.'s. The majority of the Unit M.T. came ashore during the day and the guns were in position by dusk. The airfield had been ploughed up but the R.E. parties were already at work when the Unit arrived. There was much ribald comment when the Unit's personnel contacted personnel of 2855 Squadron ex U.K., the combination of Berets, and white knees striking our "seasoned campaigners" as exceptionally humorous. Similarly the arrival of No.3230 S.C.U., the Unit with which we had done most of our training, when this Unit was already digging in was greeted with ironic cheers, the general feeling being that the R.A.F. Commandos were a "Comic Cuts" outfit.
The following vehicles arrived with the M.T. convoy:- 3-ton tenders - 13, Jeeps - 2, Motor Cycles - 5. These were allotted as follows:- 'A' Flight. 1 Jeep. 4 3-ton tenders. 1 Motor Cycle. 'B' Flight. 4 3-ton tenders. 1 Motor Cycle 'C' Flight. - ditto - H.Q.   1 Jeep. 1 3-ton tender. 1 Motor Cycle. During the night several attacks were made on the area by enemy aircraft and our guns opened up for the first time. All guns went u/s after firing a few bursts due to faulty firing cables. Signal

sent for replacements.
Sgt. KIRBY of 'A' Flight wounded in the thigh by accidental discharge of a sten carbine being cleaned by LAC. PAUL. Sgt. Kirby admitted C.C.S. and evacuated by sea. Headquarters moved from 'C' Flight to 'A' Flight at southern end of N-S runway at PACHINO.
On unloading equipment packed in M.T. it was found that there was no cooking equipment whatsoever. All cooking to be done with cut down biscuit tins. The emergency water supply, packed in M.T. in 2-gallon cans was unfit for use due to linings of cans being rusty. Fortunately supplies of water were available at the L/G.
Colonel HOWDRY and F/Lt. WHITBREAD arrived to form Headquarters, R.A.F. Regiment. LAC. ESSEX, Clk.GD and LAC. TAYLOR, Gunner-driver attached to H.Q.

16th – 31st July
2855 (LAA) Sqn – Move from Pachino Airfield north to Lentini West runway

METEOR. Weather fine. No cloud. Visibility good.
Information regarding battle situation very obscure, but there is a possibility of our moving forward to GERBINI as soon as the airfield is in our hands.
Went forward with Col. Bowdery to SIRACUSA to recce. Area prior to move. No action during the night.
METEOR. Weather fine. No cloud. Visibility good.
Information re CATANIA and GERBINI areas still somewhat obscure. Awaiting orders from Col. Bowdery to move forward.
Col. Bowdery issued orders that the Squadron move forward to CASSIBILE airfield at 09.00hrs on 18.7.43.
Warning order issued to all flight commanders. Slight air activity during the night.
METEOR. Weather fine. No cloud. Visibility good.
Instructions given to 2 i/c to bring Squadron up to R.V. West side of CASSIBILE AIRFIELD to arrive at R.V. at 11.00hrs.
Recce Group moved off for CASSIBLLE.
Contacted Major Chrisfield 75th L.A.A. Battery and Station Commander No. 244 Wing. Flight areas selected.

OPERATION 'HUSKY' – the Sicilian Campaign 1943

Sent back for "O" Group. Gun positions selected.
All guns in position. Shuttle service of vehicles operated to bring up remainder of Squadron equipment. Slight air activity during the night on shipping off beaches.
METEOR. Weather fine. No cloud. Visibility good.
Contacted S/Ldr. Disney S.L.A. No. 244 Wing. Administrative points e.g. water, rations, latrines, ablutions etc. discussed and put into operation.
Visit by Col. Bowdery. No further information regarding Battle Situation available. No activity during the night. SPECIAL NOTE. It is worth noting at this stage that during the 9 days in S.E. Sicily only once during daylight have we seen enemy aircraft. Further Squadrons arriving in this area should be equipped with Mosquito nets. Field telephones are an urgent requirement for communications.
METEOR. Weather fine. No cloud. Visibility good.
Contacted W/Cdr. Gould in AUGUSTA. Vehicles of the four Squadrons not in hand.
METEOR. Weather fine. No cloud. Visibility good.
1 Three ton Bedford lorry and 1 Motor cycle despatched for use of W/Cdr. Gould.
Visited by W/Cdr. Abrahams. Copy of War Diary up to 20.7.43 handed to him for Col. Bingham. Enemy air activity on shipping during night.
METEOR. Weather fine. No cloud. Visibility good.
Enemy activity during the night on shipping. No action on airfield
METEOR. Weather fine. No cloud. Visibility good.
Visited by Col. Salmon from N. Africa. Enemy activity during the night on shipping. No action on airfield
METEOR. Weather fine. No cloud. Visibility good.
Went forward with W/Cdr. Gould to AGNOMI airfield.
Col. Bowdery sent message with D.R. "Squadron to remain at CASSIBILE"
METEOR. Weather fine. No cloud. Visibility good.

OPERATION 'HUSKY' – the Sicilian Campaign 1943

No. 244 Wing moved forward. Instructions received from Col. Bowdery for Squadron to move to LENTINI on 28.7.43.
METEOR. Weather fine. No cloud. Visibility good.
Recce. Group moved forward to LENTINI WEST. 1 single strip to defend. Flight areas selected – one North side, 2 South side. Squadron H.Q. established with newly formed R.A.F. Regiment H.Q. at MODICA FARM one mile West of airfield.
METEOR. Weather fine. No cloud. Visibility good.
Squadron moved up. All guns in position by 14.00hrs.
Orders received from Col. Bowdery that I should form a selected Rifle Flight for special mission.
METEOR. Weather fine. No cloud. Visibility good.
Selected flight commanded by F/Lt. Farnworth with F/O. Mansfield 2nd i/c moved off to R.V. on main LENTINI – CATANIA road. Troop of armoured cars of No. 2904 Squadron attached. Liaised with Col. Cullen. MISSION. Orders given to move into CATANIA immediately it falls with S/Ldr. Griffen D.A.F.H.Q. Operational order issued to F/Lt. Farnworth by S/Ldr. Griffen.
METEOR. Weather fine. No cloud. Visibility good.
Conference held by Col. G.D. Bowdery M.C. at R.A.F. Regiment H.Q. forming new R.A.F. Regiment Group of 2 Wings. Present: L/Col. Bowdery. W/Cdr. R.E.H. Gould. S/Ldr. Chapman (2857) S/Ldr. Smith (2856) S/Ldr. Vidler (2859) S/Ldr. Kinchett (2855) S/Ldr. Adderly (2858) F/Lt. Walker (2925) and F/Lt. Barrett (2904)

2925 (LAA) Sqn – Move from Pachino and operational at Lentini East Landing Ground

Unit moved from PACHINO to LENTINI EAST. This L.G. has been cleared out of the reeds on the edge of the Lake Lentini and is alive with mosquitos. We were unable to dig in the guns as water was found a few feet down. As there were no mosquito nets among the Unit equipment all personnel suffered from the mosquitos. A few bivouacs with nets were held. Transport sent to 40 A.S.P. for nets

Squadron Headquarters moved to a farm house on the crest of one of the hills overlooking the L.G. on the west side of the L.G. 'A' Flight to the northern end of the new N-S runway, 'B' Flight to a position mid-way between the two runways and 'C' Flight with the M.T. Section, took up position in the aircraft dispersal area on the southern side of the E-W runway.

A telephone line was laid between H.Q. and 'C' Flight but the Unit had insufficient wire to put the other two Flights on the line. Wire demanded on 40 A.S.P.

Wing Commander GOULD established an R.A.F. Regiment Wing Headquarters with 322 Wing. A party line laid between Wing H.Q., 2906 Squadron and this Unit.

OPERATION 'HUSKY' – the Sicilian Campaign 1943

No.2855 Sqn Ground Defence Operational Order - Lentini West

SECRET.

No. 2855 SQUADRON, R.A.F. REGIMENT.

GROUND DEFENCE OPERATION ORDER No. 1 – LENTINI WEST AIRFIELD.

1. INTENTION.
   To defend LENTINI WEST landing ground against attack by airborne or parachute troops. In particular to prevent the destruction of aircraft or vita; R.A.F. Installations.

2. FORCES AVAILABLE.
   No. 157 Battery L.A.A.
   "A" Troop No. 158 L.A.A. Battery.
   No. 2855 Squadron A.A. R.A.F. Rgt.
   No. 2904 Squadron Field R.A.F. Rgt.
   No. 244 Wing R.A.F.

3. METHOD.
   Each Hispano Gun Position will be converted into a strong point. Slit trenches will be dug adjacent to the gun positions and sited to cover the landing ground with small arms fire. Flight Commanders will lay down arcs of fire to ensure that our own troops and aircraft are not shot up. Guns will engage in an A.A. role as long as air attack continues. All personnel surplus to gun detachments, including Flight H.Q. will man the strong point. Fire will be reserved until identification is positive.
   Squadron H.Q. Flight, with the Squadron Adjutant in command, will be responsible for the defence of the Squadron H.Q. and Regimental H.Q. The area will be defended as a strong point, slit trenches being tactically sited. A mobile patrol of 1 N.C.O. and 10 airmen, under the command of W/O Crosse will be formed and will assemble at the Adjutant's lorry. They will seek and destroy enemy in the immediate vicinity of Squadron H.Q.

4. WARNING.
   One RED signal cartridge fired in the direction of the enemy point of attack. This warning will be given by night only. All Flight Commanders including H.Q. Flight will be in possession of a signal pistol, and will give warning if necessary.

5. **COMMUNICATIONS.**
   Line communications via 244 Wing and Regimental H.Q. D.R. and runner.

6. All Flight Commanders are to be fully conversant with the Defence Scheme for the airfield.

                                                  Flight Lieutenant, Commanding,

                                                  No. 2855 Squadron, R.A.F. Regt.

6th. August, 1943.

OPERATION 'HUSKY' – the Sicilian Campaign 1943

Follow Up Phase - JULY 1943

Background

The first two weeks of July saw the four units from the U.K. at sea. Whilst harboured near Malta, all were eager to touch firm ground, having spent quite a time on board ship, but to no avail. Following a morning of enemy bombing raids on shipping, it wasn't until the afternoon of the 19th July, the L.A.A. squadrons disembarked from the troopship H.M.T. Ormonde at the port of Augusta, Sicily.

The units had to dig in around the assembly areas as they waited for news on vehicles and equipment, whilst being bombed by enemy aircraft. News came confirming that shipping sunk in the port included M.T. transporters carrying squadron vehicles and equipment. It was also confirmed that for safety reasons, other ships carrying squadron vehicles and equipment, had returned to Malta.

Following a Regiment commander conference though, lorries where promised to transport the units to their respective landing grounds. The ship carrying 2856 L.A.A. Squadron's vehicles and equipment had returned to Malta, so its role was restricted to providing static guards and patrols protecting the A.H.Q. of 211 Group at Lentini. Loaned lorries from 322 Wing H.Q. transported 2857 L.A.A. Squadron to Lentini East landing ground, where they provided anti-paratrooper protection, until their vehicles and equipment could be offloaded and collected from the port.

Although 2858 L.A.A. Squadron was transported to Lentini West landing ground and quickly took occupation, news came that their vehicles would soon be available to collect from Amber Beaches south of Syracuse. With the loss of 14 Hispano cannons, a significant number of 3 ton lorries and most of the unit's equipment, 2859 L.A.A. Squadron moved slowly to Lentini East landing ground. Although a small number of lorries where to be collected from the port of Syracuse, it was ordered to move San Francesco landing ground, by the end of the month.

The two field squadrons from Egypt, disembarked on the 24th July at the port of Syracuse. All the vehicles and equipment of 2906 Field Squadron were collected, fuelled and moved off in convoy to Lentini West landing ground. One section of A.F.V.'s were ordered to form part of a composite flight, undertaking special duties at Catania. An enemy bombing raid sunk the M.T. ship carrying 2906 Field Squadrons vehicles and equipment, losing all but 4 A.F.V.'s. The squadron was moved to Lentini East landing ground, where it mounted guards on aircraft disposal areas.

Wing Commander Gould and Lieutenant Colonel Bowdery confirmed the command structure of the R.A.F. Regiment units, introducing "informal" Wings that would command a number of squadrons. Under the command of Lieutenant Colonel Bowdery, "A" Wing would consist of 2855, 2858, 2904 and 2906 squadrons, with its H.Q. at Lentini West. Wing Commander Gould would command "B" Wing, consisting of 2856, 2857, 2859 and 2925 squadrons, with its H.Q. at 322 Wing H.Q.

Map showing the squadron positions at the end of July 1943

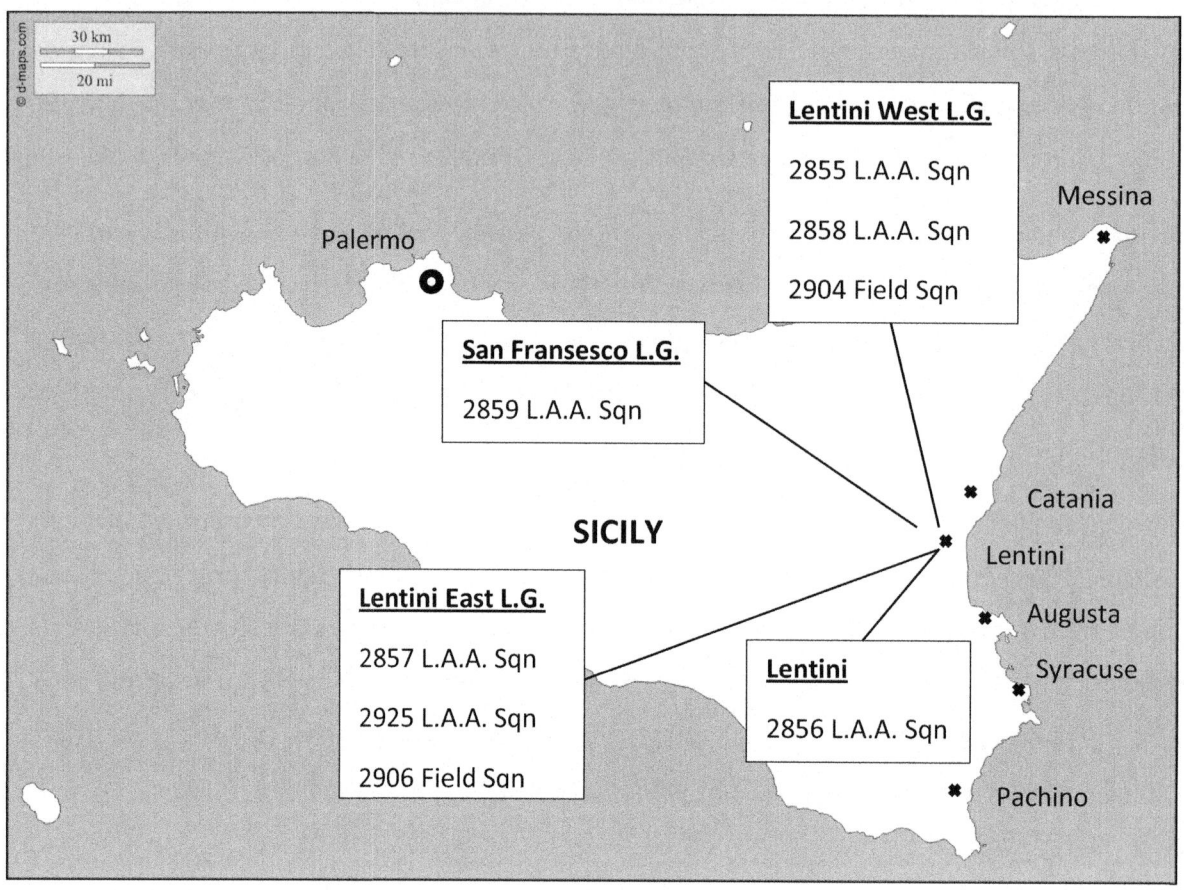

(Source: Author Adapted http://d-maps.com/m/europa/italia/sicile/sicile15.gif)

OPERATION 'HUSKY' – the Sicilian Campaign 1943

Operational Diaries

1st – 15th July
2856 (LAA) Sqn – Embarked from the U.K. with planned disembarkation at Catania

The voyage continued without incident and training was organised as far as space on board the ship would allow. The ships cinema was used on several occasions when films were shown, dealing with Aircraft Recognition and Hygiene and Sanitation. Boat Stations Parade was used daily for the purpose of a continual check of all items of personal equipment. P.T. every afternoon kept all ranks in a high state of physical fitness. This unit took part in the social activities organised on board meeting with particular success in the boxing tournament organised by F/Lt. MILLS who ably carried out the duties of ships Sports Officer.
The news of the Allied Invasion of SICILY was heard and this gave all ranks a clue to their destination.
All ranks listened to an order of the day General MONTGOMERY issued.
A meeting was held in the ship's Cinema when we were informed of our destination – SICILY. We are bound for MALTA to go into SICILY when sent for. The broad outlines of the plan are unfolded. A lecture is also given on the geographical features of the island.
Boats Stations Parade when the operation was explained to Squadron personnel. All were keenly interested and seemed to be very pleased with the news.
W/Cdr. GOULD gave a lecture in the Ship's cinema to N.C.O's and Army and R.A.F. Officers on the functions of the R.A.F. Regiment.
The Commanding Officer held a conference in his cabin, as a result of having collected his sealed orders during the morning. Maps of SICILY were obtained for the Squadron's use.
All British currency is exchanged for British Military Authority Notes. Pamphlets on ITALY are drawn for the Squadron – an interesting booklet.
The Commanding Officer issued orders concerning the operation to Flight Commanders and explained that this unit was to land at CATANIA and defend Airfields in the GERBINI Group.

OPERATION 'HUSKY' – the Sicilian Campaign 1943

2857 (LAA) Sqn – Embarked from the U.K., harboured up at Malta

En-trained from Princess Docks Liverpool, embarked on H.T. "Ormonde". All ranks in high spirits at the thought of the coming adventure.
H.T. "Ormonde" fully loaded moored into midstream. Airmen find the slinging of a hammock somewhat of a mystery.
Set sail from Liverpool, destination a mystery, everyone quite certain they knew where the ship was bound for. Arrived in the Clyde that evening, a huge convoy already assembled there. Scotsmen all keen to explain the broken coastline. Custom officials came on board during the 20/6/43.
Convey set sail, troops clustered the decks and all secretly bid farewell to "Blighty". Troops sighted S "Queen Mary" at approx: 07.50hrs, soon overtook and raced past our own ship. Below deck life beginning to become somewhat trying for the men. Food very good little complaint.
Troops permitted to wear Khaki drill shirts and shirts by day. Cinema shows and lectures very helpful to the men re tropical conditions etc.
Airmen more cheerful now as quite a number were allowed to sleep on deck, hammocks almost mastered.
Ship passed "Europa Point" at 02.30hrs. Much speculation as we entered the Mediterranean. Weather perfect, and airmen taking full advantage of spare time to sunbathe. Few cases of seasickness. Food still good.
Sailed into the harbour of Algiers, everyone expected to be allowed to disembark if only to stretch their legs. Rumoured that ship was sailing that day. Anchor up and away ay 22.00hrs.
Wireless announced the invasion of Sicily. All on board were left no doubt as to their destination. Eager to enter into the conflict.
Malta sighted quite early, entered the boom at 07.00hrs. Troops very disheartened at the fact of not being allowed ashore. Swimming would have helped the men to forget this. Much air activity over the island. Bum boats alongside, people begging for bread, our own supply getting low and not to eatable.

OPERATION 'HUSKY' – the Sicilian Campaign 1943

2858 (LAA) Sqn – Embarked from the U.K.

Unit embarked at Princess Dock, Liverpool on Ship H.M.T. Ormonde.

2906 (Field) Sqn – Embarking at the port of Alexandria, Egypt

Training continued. Received orders to move to 24 P.T.C. on 7th July 1943. H.Q. R.A.F. M.E. MS. 58775/S. Mov. S.O. dated 5th July 1943.
Precautions made for Unit movement.
Squadron moved to 24 P.T.C. Departed Shallufa 08.00hrs by train, arrived 24 P.T.C. at 19.00hrs.
C.O. and 2nd i/c visited the V.M.P. at Amryia to contact F/O Humberstone
F/O Humberstone reported from V.M.P Amryia and returned the same day. Embarkation of Squadron M.T. commenced.
F/O Humberstone & 15 drivers reported from VMP Amryia. Armoured Cars have been embarked.

16th – 31st July
2856 (LAA) Sqn – Disembarked at August harbour, moved to protect A.H.Q. 211Group at Lentini

Orders were received from Officer Commanding Troops for the disembarkation of all personnel the following day.
Squadron Personnel drew their arms from the ships armoury.
All kit bags were stacked on Port side of "C" deck.
Life-belts and vomit bags were issued as the unit was to go ashore in landing craft.
Rations were issued for the first day ashore. 2 unsuccessful bombing attacks by the enemy were experienced.
H.M.T. ORMONDE entered AUGUSTA harbour and all personnel had dinner.
All R.A.F. personnel went to their disembarkation stations. F/O. J.S. EACOTT, Squadron Adjutant was detailed as Unit Landing Officer for the R.A.F. Regiment Squadrons.
Unit Landing Officers entered the first L.C.I. and ashore. All the L.C.I's were very crowded and there seemed to be a lack of staff and organisation ashore, as a result of which kit bags of the Squadrons

OPERATION 'HUSKY' – the Sicilian Campaign 1943

became mixed which led to considerable inconvenience.
The Squadron formed up on the quay and marched to "B" Assembly Area which proved to be in several orchards near a large oil dump.
Squadron H.Q. established and Flight areas selected.
Baggage party arrived with the remainder of the unit stores from the ship. During the night there was a raid on AUGUSTA HARBOUR, shrapnel falling in the Squadron area as a result of the heavy A.A. Barrage.
Slit trenches were dug for protection against flak and Flight areas were completed. The Commanding Officer went to a conference at R.A.F. Regiment Wing H.Q. As the Squadrons vehicles had not yet been landed there was a shortage of entrenching tools, cooking equipment all of which was overcome by the excellent work of scrounging parties and improvisation. The food situation was difficult due to the small issue made from the troop sip but this was partially overcome by using the abundant supply of fruit and tomatoes which were growing in the vicinity.
Another heavy raid on AUGUSTA -shrapnel rained down on the Assembly Area and two bombs fell very close. No casualties to Squadron personnel.
The Commanding Officer received orders for troops in the Transit Area from 151 Sub-Area H.Q. It was learned that the ships transporting the Squadron's vehicles and equipment had returned to MALTA, consequently there seemed little likelihood of the unit being able to fulfil its operational role in the immediate future.
Another heavy raid on AUGUSTA but no casualties sustained by this unit.
The Commanding Officer moved forward towards the front line in the direction of CATANIA, accompanied by W/Cdr. Gould and the three other R.A.F, Regiment Squadron Commanders.
The food situation was relieved as Compo Rations were issued to the unit.
Enemy aircraft were over AUGUSTA HARBOUR bombing and machine gunning.
The Commanding Officer returned having visited AGNONE L.G., LENTINI and 211 Group A.H.Q. 151 Sub Area were contacted and promised to provide transport to move forward 2856 and 2859 Squadrons, the

OPERATION 'HUSKY' – the Sicilian Campaign 1943

former to 211 Group A.H.Q., the latter to AGNONE L.G.
Light enemy air raid on AUGUSTA and intense barrage.
Vehicle arrived from the General Transport Coy. To move the Squadron to 211 Group, A.H.Q. north of LENTINI.
5 lorries taking baggage "B" "C" and "H.Q." Flights left in convoy in that order moving via AUGUSTA, VILLASMUNDO, CARLENTINI and LENTINI to 211 Group A.H.Q. arriving at 18.15 hours.
The remainder of the Squadron under F/Lt. PEATTIE arrived, bringing bivouacs which had been obtained from 151 Sub-area. Personnel were now provided with protection against Mosquitos. Flight areas and Squadron H.Q. were chosen, bivouacs being pitched on the southern slope of a valley amongst the vines.
Patrols and listening posts mounted for protection of 211 Group A.H.Q. This Squadron is now fulfilling the role of guarding 211 Group A.H.Q. pending the arrival of its vehicles and guns which are still at MALTA. We are with most advances R.A.F. Headquarters about 8 miles behind the front line, and roughly 12 miles from CATANIA as the crow flies. The noise of bombing and artillery duels are plainly visible and a constant flow of transport passes up towards the front line along the main road.
P/O KITCHING was sent to LENTINI to contact the Town Mayor. As a result of this visit he returned with two German Field kitchens and a 200 Gallon Water tank.
Commanding Officers conference when the Defence Scheme for the area was planned. In addition to guarding 211 A.H.Q. guards were supplied for 8016 and 875 A.M.E.S.
Visit from W/Cdr. GOULD who gave the locations of other Regiment Squadrons follows 2857 Squadron – LENTINI EAST – 322 Wing. 2858 Squadron – LENTINI WEST – 322 Wing. 2859 Squadron – AGNONE L.G. – 244 Wing. 2855 Squadron – CASIBLI- 244 Wing. F/O RADWAY_MILES was detailed to return to AUGUSTA to act as R.A.F. Regiment Liaison Officer at the port in order to contact all Squadrons on the arrival of shipping bringing their vehicles and equipment. During the afternoon each Flight was taken over the ground of the surrounding district and all had a good view of the CATANIA PLAIN Battle Field.

Patrols and Listening posts mounted. Nothing of importance to report – the noise of fierce artillery duels was plainly audible from the CATANIA PLAIN area.
During the morning official mail was received from R.A.F. Regiment H.Q. giving details of nominal roles, returns and P.O.R. instructions required by Middle East Command. Patrols and listening posts mounted. Nothing further to report.
Squadron Orderly Room came into being in an organised manner. This was the first opportunity.
"A" "B" ad "C" Flights had Aircraft Recognition lectures.
A Camp Sing-Song was organised under the supervision of P/O PERRY.
Patrols and listening posts mounted – Nothing further to report.
The Squadron Adjutant visited A.H.Q., D.A.F. and obtained an Imprest Account for the Unit. Personnel were now able to receive their 1st Pay Parade since leaving the United Kingdom. Airgraphs were obtained and issue was made to all personnel complete with stamps and a Squadron Post Office was formed.
Visit from W/Cdr. GOULD who gave us the latest details regarding the location of R.A.F. Regiment units and information concerning the proposed division of Squadrons into Wings. "A" Wing under the control of Lt.Col. BOWDERY to consist of 2855, 2858, 2902 and 2904 R.A.F. Regiment Squadron with H.Q. at LENTINI WEST. "B" Wing under the control of W/Cdr. GOULD to consist of 2856, 2857, 2859 and 2925 R.A.F. Regiment Squadrons with H.Q. at 322 Wing H.Q. Information was received that the ships containing the Squadron vehicles were still at MALTA and that they were likely to be landed near SYRACUSA in a weeks time. Until then the unit was ordered to remain at its present location.
Patrols and listening posts mounted.
Practice attack alarm – all Squadron personnel standing to.
"B" Flight went on a route march the remainder having periods of Aircraft Recognition during the morning. 6 airmen were loaned to 211 Group A.H.Q Signals Unit to act as runners.
Patrols and listening posts mounted. Nothing of importance to report.
"A" Flight went on a route march the remainder having periods of

OPERATION 'HUSKY' – the Sicilian Campaign 1943

Aircraft Recognition.
The Commanding Officer and Adjutant visited A.H.Q., D.A.F. for the purpose of settling several administrative queries.
"B" Flight went on route march. A request was received for this unit to provide a guard for 6044 A.M.E.S. near VILLASMUNDO. This request was refused as the distance was too great.
Patrols and listening posts mounted. Nothing further of importance to report.
"C" Flight went on route march the remainder having period of Aircraft Recognition.
The Commanding Officer, Adjutant and Warrant Officer attended a lecture on Sanitation and Hygiene given by W/Cdr. HARVEY at 322 Wing H.Q.
Following the lecture W/Cdr. GOULD held a conference of R.A.F. Regiment Squadron Commanders, when it was learned that vehicles and equipment were likely to be landed in the near future and that a general move of units would take place. This unit received a warning order to move to AGNONE L.G. by 2nd August, 1943.
On hearing that the ship conveying this unit's vehicles and equipment was at SYRACUSA the Commanding Officer left with F/Lt. PEATTIE to visit 32c Brick Beach Unit where it was learned that the vehicles would be unloaded at 33 Brick ACID BEACH. Arrangements were made for F/Lt. PEATTIE to proceed there with drivers on August 1st. for the collection of the vehicles.
Patrols and listening posts mounted.
It was learned that 239 Wing with 5 Squadrons of Kittyhawks were to be at AGNONE L.G. The Commanding Officer and Adjutant made a reconnaissance of AGNONE L.G. for Flight areas and Squadron H.Q.
The Commanding Officer took the Flight Commanders to AGNONE L.G. for them to recce their selected Flight areas. This was found to facilitate the Squadrons movement.
During the afternoon the A.M.E.S. moved thereby enabling the patrols around 211 Group A.H.Q. to be increased. This was advantageous owing to the fact that 211 Group A.H.Q. had moved up to this location.
Patrols mounted. Nothing further of importance to report.

OPERATION 'HUSKY' – the Sicilian Campaign 1943

2857 (LAA) Sqn – Disembarked and providing guard at Lentini East Landing Ground

Set sail once again for final destination, troops received orders to draw arms and kit bags. Convoy attacked by enemy aircraft approx.: 10.30hrs. Four near misses on H.T. Ormonde. Troops shaken up a little, but it was over to quickly to disturb them very much. Entered the boom and once again attacked by aircraft, driven off by heavy barrage from warships, approx.: 11.10. Squadron third off the boat, and the landing was quite in order with little delay. Kit dumped and squadron marched to assembly area. Legs stretched for first time, Sicily did not look very appealing at that moment.
Shipping in the harbour heavily attacked by enemy Aircraft. Two ships hit, one ammunition ship which blew up at approx; 08.00hrs. Snipers very busy in vicinity.
Air attack very heavy again, shrapnel very dangerous. Morale very high, and the raids have not upset anyone. Another ship hit.
Air Attack on shipping. Troops quite used to them now.
Squadron moved to Airfield on lorries loaned by 322 Wing H.Q. Troops quite bucked at being nearer the front line.
Squadron ordered to provide static guards for protection of aerodrome against paratroops.
First lot of mail arrived for troops, mostly Air Letters, everyone happy. Food now quite regular and plentiful. News that Squadron lorries and equipment were being unloaded at Syracusa.
Four three ton lorries arrived complete with equipment aboard. Remainder still to come ashore.

2858 (LAA) Sqn – Disembarked at Port Augusta, occupying Lentini West Landing Ground

Unit disembarked at Port Augusta without casualty despite enemy bombing attack on arrival. Two E/A Macchi 202 attacked. Proceeded direct to Assembly Area "B"
Area heavily bombed by E/A. No casualties in Squadron
Area heavily bombed by E/A. One O.R. of Unit suffered minor injury from shrapnel.
Area again heavily bombed by E/A. One O.R. from M.A.R. Unit serious

injury from shrapnel - Broken Femar - Medical attention rendered by this Unit's Medical Orderlies. Airman removed to Hospital.
Carried out Recce for Forward Landing Grounds - Received orders to occupy Landing Ground Lentini West.
First supply of rations since landing received.
Area heavily bombed by E/A. No casualties sustained.
Squadron proceeded to Lentini West via Villa Mundo - Carlentini and Lentini.
Arrived Lentini West Landing Ground.
Occupation completed.
Contacted other local Units and Supplies etc.
R.A.F. Headquarters (Regt) established alongside the Unit H.Q.
R.A.F. Regiment Commander carried out Recce for Permanent H.Qs and occupied 'Modicci' 776568 Sheet 273 -1 Italy.
Sent out Patrol of 1 Officer and 9 O.R's to investigate small arms fire from Hills N.W. of airfield - Negative result.
Instructed by W/Cdr. Gould to collect Sqdn Vehicles from Amber Beaches 12 miles south of Syracuse.
Party to collect Vehicles departed from Camp.
Received orders from Regiment H.Q. to occupy Landing Ground 'Palagonia' 6658 by P.M. 1.9.43.

2859 (LAA) Sqn – Move from Lentini East to San Francesco Landing Ground

Of the Airfield that owing to conditions and also to the fact that personnel had not been issued mosquito nets, Squadron should return immediately to AUGUSTA. Owing to the lateness of the hour and that only one vehicle was available. Approximately half the party returned to AUGUSTA.
Wing Commander GOULD visited AGNONE party and gave instructions for the party at AGNONE to await further orders.
News was received today that an M.T. ship had been sunk, resulting in a loss to the Squadron of 7. 3 Ton Bedfords, 14. 20mm. Hispano Cannons, and practically the whole of the Squadron equipment. 3 Liaison Trucks were collected from SYRACUSE.
AGNONE party moved to LENTINI EAST Airfield.3. 3 Ton Bedfords were

collected from SYRACUSE.
Remainder of the Squadron moved from AUGUSTA to LENTINI EAST.
3. 3Ton Bedfords, 1 Water Tender, and 1 Liaison Truck were collected from SYRACUSE.
No.1 Flight were detached to No.151 M.U., PRIOLA for guard duties.
A lecture was given to the Squadron by Malaria Specialist of Middle East Command.
Squadron ordered to move to SAN FRANCESCO L.G. Move to be complete by 31/7/43.
No.2, 3 and Headquarters Flights move from LENTINI EAST to SAN FRANCESCO L.G.
No.1 Flight returned from No.151 M.U., PRIOLA to SAN FRANCESCO L.G. All personnel issued with mosquito nets.

2904 (Field) Sqn – Embarked from the port of Alexandria, Egypt, moved to occupy Lentini West Landing Ground

Movement order. All personnel confined to camp. 12.00. 'A' Flt. 'Armoured Flt, 6 H.Q. personnel and 4 of 'C' Flt. Moved off for embarkation on ship 'F'. (P/O LAWN and P/O BRODIE) 12.45. 'C' Flt. And 'Support' Flt. Moved off for embarkation on ship 'G' (F/O TURLEY and F/O MACMILLAN). 15.00. 3 replacements obtained from 2903 Squadron for personnel non effective sick. 16.00. H.Q. and 'B' Flts. Paraded for shipping tickets.
Reveille. 05.30. Rations issued. 06.15. C.O., Adjutant and F/O BALLIE and 67 O/R's moved by road for No.18 E.U. Arrived 07.30. 08.30 Embarked aboard S.S. Empire Trooped. 10.00. F/O BAILIE appointed 'F' Deck Mess Officer. 11.00. Adjutant visited Embarkation Paymaster re Pay Parade and exchange of currency. 14.30. Muster stations. 18.30. Pay parade held.
08.00. Sailed from Alexandria. 09.00. Muster stations.10.00. Unit's Sealed Orders opened by C.O. and discussed with Adjutant. 11.00. Supplementary Pay parade for Guards. 17.00. Arms inspection.
Adjutant visited Ship's Medical Officer, and obtained one weeks supply of Mepacrine tablets for all ranks. 14.00. Conference of all Unit C.O's. Practice Boar Drill throughout day.

OPERATION 'HUSKY' – the Sicilian Campaign 1943

Daily news sheet readout on parade. All ranks informed of object, i.e. capture of Sicily, need for certain precautions and implicit obedience of orders. Further Boat Drill.
Orders received covering disembarkation of all troops on 24th July, 1943. 48hrs rations collected.
7 Officers and 189 men disembarked at SYRACUSE. 17.00. Party arrived at 'Z' Transit Camp (No.198). All Squadron present. 18.00. Meal served, verbal orders issued regarding Daily Detail, Security, Air Raid warnings etc., and Guards mounted.
Air Raid warning. 05.00. All clear. 09.00. Parade and arms inspected. Sanitation Squad detailed to dig latrines. Routine Orders read to Squadron. 14.00. Camp site changed. 15.00 P/O LAWN returned from SYRACUSE with A.F.V's. 17.30 Rations drawn from D.I.D.
C.O. and F/O TURLEY visited SYRACUSE to ascertain when Squadron M.T. would be unloaded. 14.00. C.O. and F/O LAWN went out in one A.F.V. to recce ground at LENTINI. 19.00. Conference of all C.O's at Transit Camp Headquarters. Adjutant visited docks re unloading of M.T.
F/O BAILIE and 4 drivers proceeded to docks to assist in disembarkation of M.T. vehicles from 'S.S. Fort MAURAPAS'. 07.00. 2 Corporals and 10 drivers also proceeded to docks. C.O. and P/O LAWN returned from recce. 11.00. Transit Camp Medical Officer visited Unit to inspect sanitary arrangements, and expressed his pleasure at condition. 14.30. COL. SALMON, C.O. R.A.F. REGIMENT, visited the Unit. 19.00. F/O TURLEY returned from docks with one 15 cwt truck.
C.O. and P/O LAWN proceeded on recce AUGUSTA with one A.F.V. 08.30. F/O TURLEY proceeded to docks to supervise unloading of M.T. 13.00. C.O. and P/O LAWN returned from AUGUSTA having located 4 A.F.V's for 2906 Squadron. 14.00. All Unit M.T. already unloaded was serviced with petrol, oil and water. Transit Camp routine proceeded.
M.T. drivers proceeded to docks to complete unloading of remainder of Squadron M.T. 07.30. C.O. proceeded m/c to LENTINI to recce area for camp site. 10.00. F/O TURLEY and ADJUTANT visited docks. 14.30. WING COMMANDER GOULD visited Unit. Orders received to move to LENTINI WEST on 30th, July, 1943. 17.00. C.O. returned form LENTINI, 17.30. Warning Order issued to Flight Commanders, for move of Unit to LENTINI WEST at 07.30 hours on 30th. July. All drivers to service

OPERATION 'HUSKY' – the Sicilian Campaign 1943

vehicles and line up in convoy order by 07.00. 'Support Flight' i/c F/O TURLEY to remain as rear party in order to disembark portees and remaining M.T.
Warning received from O.C. 'Z' Transit Camp that Paratroops were expected during the night. A composite flight was warned to stand by ready for immediate disposal. Main Guard doubled and 6 extra mean detailed for M.T. Guard.
Squadron moved off in convoy, A.F.V's at head and rear to provide A/A protection. 11.30. Arrived at LENTINI WEST and laagered for Tiffin. 14.30. Unit moved into copse 200 yds. NORTH of 244 WING, adjacent to Railway Halt 258. 16.00. C.O., ADJUTANT and P/O LAWN with one section of A.F.V's reported to COL. BOWDERY at HEADQUARTERS, R.A.F. REGIMENT, Map reference: SICILY 1:50,000 Sheet 273/1 778568. P/O LAWN with one section A.F.V's detailed to rendezvous with composite flight of Regiment under command of FL/LT FARNSWORTH on LENTINI-CATANIA ROAD for special duties. 19.00. C.O. and F/O TURLEY visited Headquarters 2858 Squadron.
ADJUTANT visited S/LDR. DISNEY at 244 WING to discuss matters of Administration, Rations, Petrol etc. also the Wing Hospital re Medical Matters. 10.30 The ADJUTANT then visited S/LDR MARSHALL (S/LDR ADMIN) 322 WING. The CPO attended a conference of all Regiment Squadron Commanders at HEADQUARTERS, R.A.F. REGIMENT. F/O TURLEY and A, B and C Flight Commanders proceeded on recce of LENTINI WEST L.G. 13.30. Two 15 cwt trucks dispatched to PORT AUGUSTA for Rations and petrol. 14.30. C.O. and ADJUTANT visited HEADQUARTERS, DESERT AIR FORCE to discuss Rationing and the opening of an Imprest Account. 16.00. C.O. and AJUTANT visited D.I.D. WEST of SCORFIA on SCORDIA-PALGONIA ROAD to arrange for rations to be drawn for following day. 17.00. 30th. ARMY CORP. Petrol point was visited in an endeavour to arrange for a petrol issue. ADJUTANT was referred to 30th ARMY CORP REAR H.Q. MAIN 75 to obtain an allotment. 19.00. Conference of Officers was held, C.O. informed all officers that Squadron would take over from 2858 Squadron at 14.00. 1st. August, 1943., and would be responsible for all patrols and defence of LENTINI WEST AERODROME, as from that date. F/O TURLEY gave A, B and C, Flight Commanders their locations for respective Flight H.Q's as follows:-

Map reference ITALY 1:100,000 Sheet 273 CALTAGIRONE. S.H.Q. Map reference 794573, 'A' Flight H.Q. Map reference 816562, 'B' Flight H.Q. Map reference 794573, 'C' Flight H.Q. Map reference 813580. Respective patrol areas were all allotted and provision made for contact between Flights on all flanks. It was decided that A section of A.F.V.'s would provide day patrols, A, B& C Flights each to provide a night patrol of 1 Cpl. And 7 O.R's, in 3 hr. spells, whilst 'Support Flight' would remain in reserve at Squadron H.Q. Intercommunication would be by D/R at first, then later by R/T and Field Telephone. F.A.P. would be located at Squadron H.Q. Sick Parade at 08.15. at 92 Squadron M.I. Room. Sanitation arrangements as provided by the ADJUTANT with M.O. 92 Squadron. MESSING.H.Q. B, Armoured and Support Flights would mess at S.H.Q. A & C Flights would draw rations daily at 10.30hrs from S.H.Q. and establish independent messes, cooking utensils to be provided by S.H.Q. WATER. It was arranged that the Water Bowser would provide A & C Flights with 32 gallons of water each, daily, for drinking and cooking purposes.

2906 (Field) Sqn – Embarked from Alexandria and moved to Lentini East Landing Ground

All Squadron MT have now been embarked at Alexandria
F/O Humbrestone & 3 OR's embarked at Alexandria.
F/O Skelton, P/O Fleming & 63 OR's embarked at Alexandria. Ship "F". F/O Briten, P/O Weaver & 63 OR's embarked at Alexandria. Ship "G".
F/Lt Blackwood, F/O Davies & 60 OR's embarked at Alexandria. Ship "H". The whole Squadron & its transport now embarked, less one O.R. removed from ship to Hospital at Alexandria.
Convoy sailed at approximately 08.00hrs.
Uneventful voyage.
Arrived Syracuse at 08.00hrs. Disembarked 14.30hrs. One OR removed to Hospital. 184 OR's & 6 Officers proceeded to 198 T.C.
Air attack on harbour at approximately 04.00hrs. Ship in harbour hit and subsequently sunk. C.O. proceeded to Syracuse harbour to make enquiries concerning Squadron's Mechanical Transport, all of which, without exception of 4 Armoured Cars, were aboard ship "F.C.2". He

was informed that the ship sunk during early hours was probably "F.C.2".
It was confirmed that ship "F.C.2" had been sunk and that consequently the Squadron had lost the following:- 19 Dodges (15cwts), Water Tender (200 galls. Dodge), 2 Dodges (3 tons), 4 Chev Portees, 4 Anti-Tank Guns (2lbs), all stores & equipment of the Squadron. (The Squadron now only have 4 Armoured Cars). There were no casualties. C.O. proceeded to try and contact Lt/Col. Bowdery, in order to report to him, but failed.
Col. Salmon O.C. RAF Regt. At present in Sicily visited Squadron.
F/O Humberstone reported from Port Augusta with 4 Armoured Cars. CO visited Air Stores Park to endeavour to obtain essential equipment, more especially cooking utensils etc. One Minor Formation Store was bought back.
W/Cdr. Gould visited Squadron which will now probably come under B Wing. C.O. visited 244 Wing at Pachino.
C.O. reported to W/Cdr Gould at "B" Wing. Adjutant visited Town Major, Syracuse D.A.D.O.S. & 40 A.S.P. in search of equipment etc. No cooking utensils available. Mosquito nets and small amount of clothing obtained.
Squadron moved to Lentini East L.G. (Regimental Order No.5 Serial No.2 dated 30/7/43) to relieve No. 2857 Squadron. One Officer & 50 OR's detached to No.121 M.U. Remainder of Squadron arrived at Lentini East L.G. at approximately 16.00hrs. Guard mounted on aircraft dispersal areas.

OPERATION 'HUSKY' – the Sicilian Campaign 1943

No.2904 Sqn. Movement Order

APPENDIX 1.   SECRET

MOVEMENT ORDER NO. 2.   (COPY)

6th July, 1943.

INFORMATION.

No. 2904 Squadron will proceed from SHALLUFA Station by train on 7th July, 1943.

Conducting Officer – F/O TURLEY.

INTENTION.

To proceed to No. 24. P.T.C.

EXECUTION.

- (a) Time schedule. Reveille 04.30hrs. Breakfast 05.00hrs. Treatment at M.I. Room, 06.00hrs. Train rations for the journey will be collected from Airmen's Mess at 06.00hrs. Parade 06.30hrs. Train rations will be brought to the Squadron Orderly Room for distribution at 06.40hrs. Move off 07.00hrs. Depart SHALLUFA 08.00hrs. E.T.A. at No. 24. P.T.C. = 18.00hrs

- (b) Squadron will parade in full marching order at 06.30hrs. 7th July, 1943, at the R.A.F. Regiment Training Centre. Mess Tins must be in side haversack, and readily accessible to take train rations of the journey. Water bottle will be filled and carried at the side.

- (c) Flight Commanders will inspect their Flights and ensure that all men are present, and report to the Conducting Officer.

- (d) The baggage party will consist of Cpl. BRIMSON, and six Squadron Police. Rations will be in charge of Cpl. JOHNSON, and three AC Cooks. The Squadron Orderly Room will be in charge of Cpl. BRODIE and two AC clerks. The baggage party will constitute the advance party and will proceed with rations and baggage at 06.45hrs.

- (e) The Main Party will proceed in Station transport by flights at 07.00hrs. They will debuss outside the Station and form up in flights facing the train in the following order, A.B.C., Support and Headquarters Flights.

(f) Each flight will be told off for coaches before proceeding onto the platform.

(g) On the order being given to "entrain", the men will get into their respective coaches. Once entrained no one is to leave the train without permission from the Conducting Officer.

(h) At each recognised halting place, all officers will descend and proceed to the carriage of the men in their charge.

(i) Kits will be left under guard.

(j) On the order being given to "Fall in" and entrain the men will return to their coaches. Each officer will ensure that all his men are present, and then report to the Conducting Officer.

(k) In the event of accident, officers will proceed to the carriages of their men. Men will NOT descend unless ordered to do so.

(l) Each officer will be responsible for his own flight.

EXECUTION.

(m) On the order being given to "Detrain", by the Conducting Officer, the Flight Commanders will form in flights on the platform facing the train, in the following order - A.B.C. Support and Headquarters Flights, and await the order to move off.

(n) The baggage party will clear all baggage and rations from the train.

(o) The number of men present will be checked, and the Squadron will move off to their lines.

(p) The Squadron Orderly Officer will inspect the Airmen's Mess at 04.30hrsand 05.00hrs, on the 7th. July, 1943.

(q) Each Flight Commander will detail a runner in order to establish contact with the Conduction Officer when necessary.

ADMINISTRATION.
The Station M.T. transporting the men to the railway station will return to the R.A.F. Regiment Training Centre, after the men have debussed.

FIRST AID.
First Aid, if required, will be administered by the Nursing Orderly, who will be located with Headquarters Flight.

(Signed) C.B. BARRETT,

Flight Lieutenant, Commanding,
2904 Squadron R.A.F. Regiment,
MIDDLE EAST.

OPERATION 'HUSKY' – the Sicilian Campaign 1943

No.2904 Field Squadron Establishment

WAR ESTABLISHMENT OF A FIELD SQUADRON (RAF REGIMENT)

Establishment No. LWE/ME/2015   Date 10th. May 1943   Authority; MS 58716/Est.

DETAIL.	OFFICERS				AIRMEN				
	S/L.	F/L.	F/O	TOTAL	W/O	F/Sgt.	Sgt.	Cpl.	ACs.	TOTAL.
HEADQUARTERS										
(a) RAF Regiment.	1	1	1	3				1	1	2
Clerks (General Duties)								1	3	4
Cooks.									1	1
Equipment Assistants.							1		1	2
Fitters M.T.								1		1
Fitters Armourer Guns								1		1
(b) Gunners.							1	1	16	19
Medical Nursing Orderlies.					1			2	1	3
M.T. Mechanics.									1	1
Wireless Operators Mechanics								1	1	2
TOTAL HEADQUARTERS.	1	1	1	3	1		2	8	24	35
3 RIFLE FLIGHTS.										
RAF Regiment.			3	3						
(c) Gunners.							3	9	96	108
TOTAL 3 RIFLE FLIGHTS.			3	3			3	9	96	108
ARMOURED FLIGHT.										
R.A.F. Regiment.			1	1						
(d) Gunners							1	1	12	16
TOTAL ARMOURED FLIGHT.			1	1			1	1	12	16
SUPPORT FLIGHT.						1	1	2	26	30
Gunners.						1	1	2	26	30
TOTAL SUPPORT FLIGHT						1	1	2	26	30
TOTAL SQUADRON	1	1	5	7	1	1	8	21	158	189

REMARKS.
(a) Includes:- 2nd in Command and Officer i/c 1 F/Lt, Support Flt. Adjutant 1 F/O
(b) Signallers 3 ACs, Despatch Riders 2 ACs, Drivers 3 ACs, Sqdn. Police. 1 Cpl. 6 ACs
(c) Includes;- Drivers 3 ACs per flt.
(d) Includes;- AFV Crew 2 Sgts. 2 Cpls. 10 ACs. Despatch Riders 2 ACs.

WAR ESTABLISHMENT OF A FIELD SQUADRON (RAF REGIMENT)

(ii) MECHANICAL TRANSPORT.

PRIME MOVERS.	Sqdn.H.Q.	3 Rifle Flights.	Armoured Flt.	Support Flight.	Total.
AFVs.	–	–	5	–	5
Cycles Motor	2	3	2	2	9
Tenders, 3 ton.	–	–	–	5	5
Vans 15cwt.	6	12	–	1	19
TOTAL PRIME MOVERS.	8	15	7	8	38
OTHER VEHICLES.					
Trailer. Water 150Galls.	1	–	–	1
TOTAL OTHER VEHICLES.	1	–	–	–	1

NOTE 1. The above establishment is applicable to the following RAF Regiment Squadrons;-

    No. 2904 Squadron.

    No. 2906 Squadron.

"A" Wing - AUGUST 1943
Overview

With limited Hispano cannons and a flight still on special duties in Catania, 2855 L.A.A. Squadron at Lentini West landing ground, experimented with a revised structure of two operational flights with 8 cannons each. The squadron sustained its first casualties of the operation on the 11th August, when a heavy Axis raid by around 20 Junker 88 bombers, caused significant damage on the landing ground, killing two airmen. Although there was a claim on damaging an enemy aircraft, it's submission to authorities was made impossible, immediately after the raid, as all personnel were engaged in firefighting activities.

The move of 2858 L.A.A. Squadron, north of Catania, from Lentini West to the Palagonia landing ground, proved to be relatively uneventful for the rest of the month.

The guarding of requisitioned assets in Catania, and the securing of equipment was handed over to 2904 Field Squadron, relieving 2855 L.A.A. Squadron. The field squadron spent the remainder of the month guarding the assets in the town, rotating their rifle flights and guarding the aerodrome using both their A.F.V. and Support Weapons flights.

Map showing the 'A' Wing Units at the end of August 1943

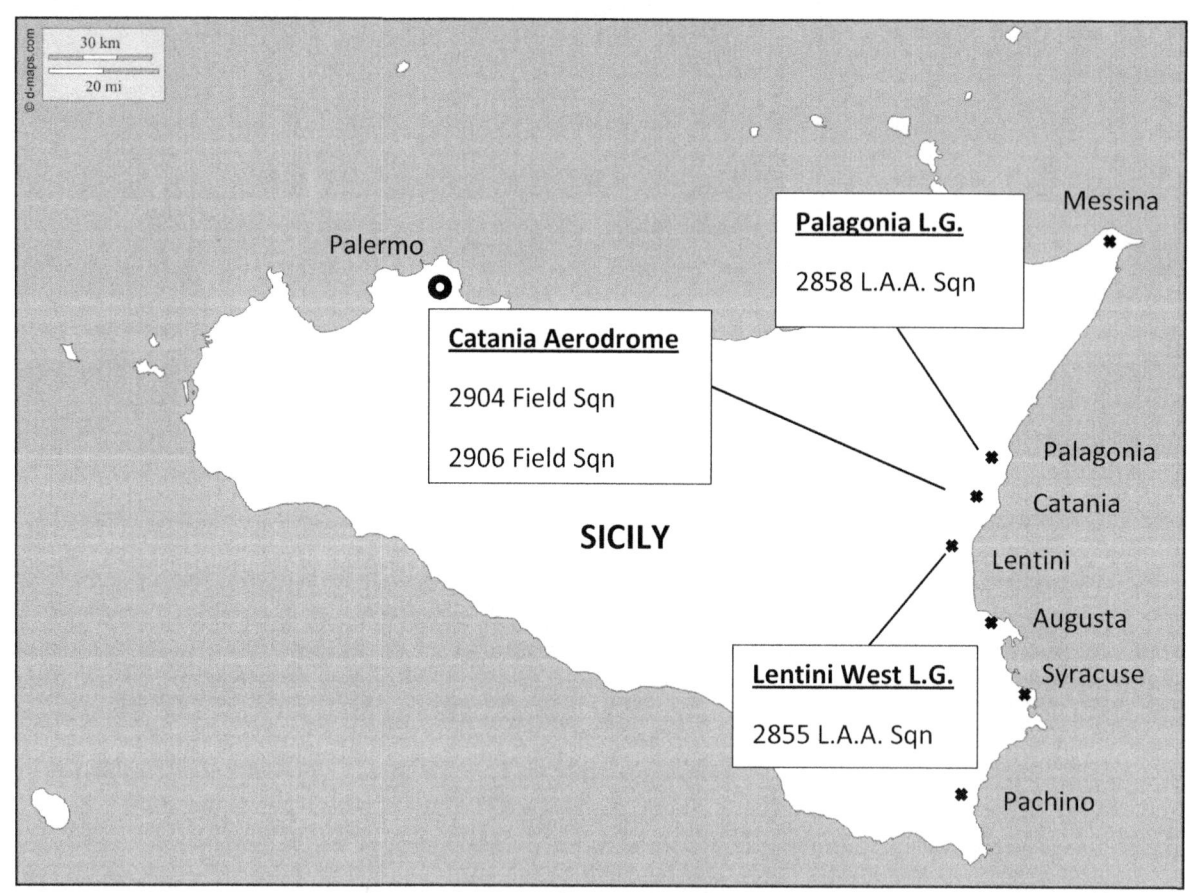

(Source: Author Adapted http://d-maps.com/m/europa/italia/sicile/sicile15.gif)

The first week of the month saw 2906 Field Squadron providing ground defence of the Lentini East landing ground, but they were soon ordered to move north, to seal and protect Catania aerodrome. Its immediate primary role was to prevent the removal or destruction of aircraft, equipment, stores and papers etc., which would prove valuable to the Intelligence units. This proved not to be the easiest of tasks, as a main road ran through the middle of the aerodrome. Near the end of the month a detachment from the squadron was also sent out to Messina, to guard building of importance.

OPERATION 'HUSKY' – the Sicilian Campaign 1943

Operational Diaries

1st – 15th August
2855 (LAA) Sqn – Operational at Lentini West Landing Ground

METEOR. Weather fine. No cloud. Visibility good.
Flight Lieutenant T.J. Tarry assumed command of No.2855 Squadron vice S/Ldr. H.F. Kinchett detached on special Wing Duties. Authority: Lt/Col. Bowdery M.C. R.A.F. Regt.
METEOR. Weather fine. No cloud. Visibility good.
Airfield Ground Defence Conference held at A.H.Q. (Map. Reference Sicily Sheet 273 751535). It was decided that the basis for ground defence would be: 1. Static defence of gun positions which could be converted into strong points. 2. Formation of mobile troops consisting of army A.A. Units and R.A.F. Regiment personnel from H.Q. Staffs. 3. 3. Sitting of L.M.Gs with co-ordinated arcs of fire.
METEOR. Weather fine. No cloud. Visibility good.
Received standing orders for Ground Defence from Lt/Col. Ian Bowater, Commanding 53rd L.A.A. Regt.
Contacted 244 Wing R.A.F. (S/Ldr. Disney) and discussed the scheme in outline and was instructed in the defence requirements of the Wing. Basis decided was that Regt. personnel would defend statically, their own aircraft and installations and that movement would be reduced to a minimum. Warning signal (One Red from Very Pistol) was agreed. S/Ldr. Disney reiterated his view that in addition to manning guns R.A.F. Regiment A.A. Squadron should act in a liaison capacity between Army A.A. Units and R.A.F. Wing H.Q.
Received information from F/Lt. H. Farnworth i/c Special Flight, that No. 130266 L.A.C. Ingham H. (Gunner D.R.) had been missing since 19.00hrs 3.8.43. After considerable search this airman was located at No. 7 C.C.S. he had received injuries in a road accident, but was unable to give any coherent account of the accident and did not know what had become of his motor cycle.
Received information from F/Lt. H. Farnworth (Special Flight) that entry into CATANIA appeared imminent.
Visited Special Flight. Contacted S/Ldr. Griffen i/c R.A.F. Recce

Party.
METEOR. Weather fine. No cloud. Visibility good.
Received draft defence scheme from Major Roberts and completed detail.
Received message from Special Flight that one section plus one Armoured Car had proceeded into CATANIA.
Received message from Special Flight that remainder of party had proceeded to CATANIA at 18.00hrs.
METEOR. Weather fine. No cloud. Visibility good.
Operation Order No.1 issued to Squadron for Airfield Defence. Received message that Special Flight had established themselves in CATABIA at 20.00hrs 5.8.43 at S.I.T.A. Works, Via Roccaromano.
METEOR. Weather fine. No cloud. Visibility good.
Received completed Defence Scheme from Major Roberts.
Arrived in CATANIA and contacted Special Flight. Inspected buildings that had been requisitioned. Entry had been forced before Flight's arrival and considerable damage and disorder was apparent. Guards were mounted from 12.00hours 5.8.43 and had been maintained continuously. This flight was too small for the increasing commitments and I therefore requested the Commander R.A.F. Regiment to arrange for their relief.
Message sent to Special Flight ordering them to hand over to No.2904 Squadron by 09.00hrs 8.8.43. Information received from No.3232 S.C. R.A.F. that they were in possession of M.T. cycle No.83887. Vehicle was beyond repair and rear wheel had been removed to put into service a motor cycle belonging to that unit. The remains of the motor cycle were collected and brought back to this unit.
METEOR. Weather fine. No cloud. Visibility good.
Special Flight reported to Squadron H.Q. having been relieved at CATANIA.
S/Ldr. Disney of No.244 Wing visited this H.Q. to discuss a general plan of Defence of Advanced Landing Grounds. The basis was to produce a key plan which would be applicable to all Advanced Landing Grounds, both from an A.A. and Ground Defence angle. The necessity for an A.A. Squadron, R.A.F. Regiment to be attached to

OPERATION 'HUSKY' – the Sicilian Campaign 1943

the Wing was again stressed. It was suggested that the A.A. Squadron should be on the Landing Ground a few hours in advance of the Wing, and should be prepared to inform the Wing of the state of defences on its arrival.
METEOR. Weather fine. No cloud. Visibility good.
Received report from Special Flight on their activities in CATANIA.
METEOR. Weather fine. No cloud. Visibility good.
Consequence upon the loss of eight Hispano A.A. Guns at sea, the Squadron was experimentally re-organised as follow: Two operational flights each with 49 personnel plus one officer, manning 8 A.A. Guns each. M.T. Section H.Q.
METEOR. Weather fine. No cloud. Visibility good.
Airfield heavily attacked by enemy aircraft (J.U 88) estimated to number about 20 in bright moonlight. One E.A. claimed to be damaged by our guns, but owing to the fact that all personnel were engaged in fighting fires immediately after the raid, it was impossible to submit a claim to the A.A.D.C. in sufficient time for consideration. The unit suffered two casualties by bomb splinters and they were removed to No.4 C.C.S. LENTINI WEST LANDING GROUND 1355517 A/Cpl. Rogerson W. (Gunner 5) 1809081 A.C.1. Newman G. (Gunner 5) See action report for full details of raid. Ammunition expenditure: 857 rounds 20m.m.
METEOR. Weather fine. No cloud. Visibility good.
No.1355517 A/Cpl. Rogerson W. (Gunner 5) died of wounds received in action on 11.8.43.
Attended A.A. Conference at No.157 Battery H.Q. Defences had been improved by additional 10 Bofors, making 36 in all, together with 12 heavy guns in the immediate vicinity. Umbrella barrage was arranged to be centred over the middle of the airfield. No.2855 Squadron guns to fire the barrage under the control of the Bofor Master-Gun.
A party consisting of 15 men and one three ton lorry from Squadron

OPERATION 'HUSKY' – the Sicilian Campaign 1943

H.Q. detailed to stand by for Fire Fighting purposes. To proceed to Landing Ground immediately after the conclusion of any raid to assist ground personnel to deal with any fire still burning. No. 1355517 A/Cpl. Rogerson W. (Gunner 5) buried in SCORDIA CEMETARY. M.R. SCORDIA H.7455 SHEET 56.
No. 1809081 A.C.1. Newman G. (Gunner 5) died at No.4 C.C.S. SCORDIA of wounds received in action on 11.8.43.
METEOR. Weather fine. No cloud. Visibility good.
No.1809081 A.C.1. Newman G. (Gunner 5) buried at LENTINI WEST LANDING GROUND Plot No.11. M.R. ITALY SCORDIA SHEET 273 IM 814573.
METEOR. Weather fine. No cloud. Visibility good.
Message received from B.P.O H.Q.M.E. that the six airman reported missing at sea in Ship B.B.3 on 5.7.43 had landed safely at ALGIERS and left 39 P.T.C. on 12.8.43 to rejoin this unit.
Attended conference at R.A.F. Regiment H.Q. called by Lt/Col. C.D. Bowdery M.C. General regiment policy and equipment deficiencies were discussed in detail.

2858 (LAA) Sqn – Move from Lentini West Runway to Palagonia Landing Ground

Squadron proceeded from Lentini West Landing Ground to Palagonia Landing Ground (79th Fighter Group, U.S.A.A.F. operating from this L.G.). Transport incomplete not having been unloaded from ships in time for move of Squadron.
Squadron vehicles having been unloaded at Syracuse, W/O. Rastall and party of airmen convoyed vehicles to Palagonia, arriving with all vehicles at 18.00hrs.
Commanding Officer 79th Group, U.S.A.A.F. invited Squadron to make use of cinema shows held by the U.S.A.A.F. Squadrons on the Landing Ground.
114675 F/O. (A/F/Lt) Ball, S.M. admitted to No.3 C.C.S. Posted non-effective sick w.e.f. same date.
Squadron Adjutant attended Conference at R.A.F. Regiment Headquarters.
First issues from N.A.A.F.I. purchased since landing in Sicily, greatly appreciated by the personnel of this Squadron.

OPERATION 'HUSKY' – the Sicilian Campaign 1943

Sent patrol out to area South of Landing Ground to investigate statement by Sicilian to the effect that German Paratroops were in the area, with negative results. The Patrol consisted of F/Lt. Hickinbotham, D.P. and 9 airmen.

First private mail received from U.K. since embarking on present operation.

Commanding Officer attended Conference of Squadron Commanders at R.A.F. Regiment H.Q.

2904 (Field) Sqn – Move to Catania town and aerodrome

Adjutant proceeded to D.I.D. West of Scordia to arrange collection of 48hrs. rations. He then proceeded to 30th Corps Main 75, in an endeavour to arrange petrol allotment.

The Squadron commenced move to new location using Squadron M.T. 11.00. A & C Flights in position. 11.30. Armoured, Support, HQ and B Flights in position. Disposition of flights at S.H.Q. were as follows. B Flight lines East of Wadi running West to East towards Landing Ground. Support, Armoured and HQ Flights West of B lines. Squadron Personnel employed on fatigues in camp lines. Cookhouse erected, ammo and petrol pits dug. 17.00. C.O. and F/O Turley visited A & C Flight camp sites. 19.00 Conference of Officers held to discuss matters arising out of the day's work. In view of warning received, precautions taken against Paratroops. 21.00. Field telephone line tested with H.Q. R.A.F. Regiment, through 244 Wing.

C.O. visited F/Lt. Blackwood, O.C.2906 Squadron. 10.30. S/Ldr. Disney visited with F/O Turley. 08.30. 2 Field Telephones and 2 coils wire issued to Wing Commdr. Gould, O.C. "B" Wing, on temporary loan. 14.30. Adjutant visited Accountant Officer 244 Wing to obtain cash for Pay Parade. 15.00. C.O. visited S/Ldr. Disney to discuss aerodrome Defence scheme. 15.15. Pay Parade held at S.H.Q. for Support and Armoured Flights. 16.00. S/Ldr. DISNEY requested a Guard of 1 Cpl. & 6 O.R's at night on R.S.U. at Lentini West. This was arranged. 17.00. Landing Ground Patrols by A, B, C, Flights as detailed from dusk to dawn.

Adjutant attended conference of all Squadron Adjutants at HQ,

OPERATION 'HUSKY' – the Sicilian Campaign 1943

R.A.F. Regiment. Support Flight – Gun drill 08.30 – 12.00. 14.30. Adjutant visited D.A.F. to obtain Imprest Account, and also visited A.P.O. Francesco, but no mail was yet forthcoming. 17.00. C.O. attended conference on Airfield Ground Defence at area A/A H.Q. M.P. Sheet 273 751535. F/O BAILIE & F/O TURLEY visited B.I.S. at port Augusta and obtained £50 supplies.
Medical Officer of 92 Squadron inspected sanitary arrangements. 10.00. F/O HUMBERSTON 2906 Squadron visited Unit to return one Motor Cycle U/S. 10.30. Adjutant 244 Wing requested that a guard be provided on the runway to prevent traffic crossing the Landing Ground instead of using the track. P/O BRODIE was detailed to liaise with Wing Operations, recce the position and render a report to the C.O. 11.30. O.C. 2855 Squadron visited C.O. to discuss Aerodrome Defence Scheme. 14.00. C.O. & F/O TURLEY went out on recce to West of Lentini. 19.00. Request from 244 Wing Operations F/O STUART to mount crash guard on Spitfire at H7865 S.E. corner of Garbini 7. Confirmation having been obtained from F/Lt. WHITBREAD, HQ, R.A.F. Regiment, an A.F.V. was sent out with 48 hrs rations.
Request from HQ, RAF Regiment that C.O. would be going out to that area on a recce this a.m. 09.30. Adjutant visited Field Cashier at Desert Air Force. 12.25. Lt.Col. BOWDERY and F/Lt. WHITBREAD visited the Squadron Headquarters. 12.30. P/O BRODIE reported on proceedings of Hygiene Lecture at 244 Wing Medical Centre. 12.45. O.C. 2855 Squadron visited Unit to discuss drome defence scheme.
C.O Reported to LT.COL. BOWDERY on conditions at GERBINI district. All airfields pattern bombed and deserted. Probably mined off tracks. No stores or serviceable equipment, all probably burnt or destroyed. Airfield Construction Unit at present at work on fields. 14.00. Pay Parade.
C.O. proceeded to GERBINI to arrange collection of crashed spitfire. 18.00. C.O. attended conference at HQ, BOFORS, with MAJOR ROBERTS re ground defence scheme. Wing Commander Padre visited Unit and a Church Parade was arranged for 09.00hrs. on 8th August, 1943. S/Ldr. Roman Catholics Padre visited Unit. 14.00. Wing Armament Officer visited Unit with F/LT PRESSTAGE. The use of the 25yrd range was obtained on 7th. August, for practice by the

OPERATION 'HUSKY' – the Sicilian Campaign 1943

Unit. 17.45. ADJUTANT phoned F/LT. TENDICK, Signals Officer 244 Wing, re Unit R/T Frequency of 5450 Kcs. 18.00. C.O. attended Wing Conference.
C.O. went on recce with Squadron Commanders "A" Wing. 14.00. ADJUTANT visited C.S.O. Rear Headquarters, Desert Air Force re allotment of R/T Frequency for A.F.V's and TR9D's. The C.S.O. referred the ADJUTANT to F/LT. BONNER, who allotted the Squadron a frequency of 6020Kc's. It was arranged that quartz plates would be forthcoming if possible from 211 Group. 17.00. C.O. returned from recce of CATANIA with all Squadron Commanders and LT.COL. BOWDERY. Order received by C.O. from LT.COL. BOWDERY to proceed to CATANIA and guard various installations and buildings requisitioned for R.A.F. 19.00. HQ and A Flight moved off in convoy for CATANIA, with C.O. ADJUTANT & P/O BRODIE. F/O TURLEY left behind as I/C Rear Party, with Support, Armoured, B & C Flights and F/O MACMILLAN & F/O BALLIE.
Convoy arrived at SITA GARAGE. P/O LAWN reported present conditions to C.O., with F/O MANSFIELD of 2855 Squadron.
C.O., ADJUTANT and F/O MANSFIELD inspected block of flats and requisitioned buildings from the TOWN MAYOR to serve as Squadron H.Q. and billets for personnel. 08.30. C.O. and F/O MANSFIELD visited buildings and installations already requisitioned for R.A.F. with the view to taking over guard duties from 2855 Squadron. Fatigues parties organised to clear S.H.Q. building for occupation as billets for HQ and two sections of A Flight. 10.00. F/O TURLEY and rear party reported to S.H.Q. Support and Armoured Flights were detailed to proceed to CATANIA AIRFIELD, to patrol and guard existing installations and equipment in liaison with F/LT.BLACKWOOD, C.O. 2906 Squadron. B & C Flights were allotted various works and buildings to guard, all previously requisitioned for R.A.F. 11.00. F/LT WHITBREAD visited Unit. 12.00. The undermentioned buildings having been requisitioned through the TOWN MAJOR at CATANIA and held for DAF and RAF REGIMENT, the guard on these buildings was taken over by the Unit at 12.00. under instructions from LT.COL. BOWDERY, HEADQUARTERS, RAF REGIMENT. (1). Store house containing barrack furniture, 133, VAI FRANCESCO CRISPI. (2). FIAT GARAGE & REPAIR SHOP. (3). HOSPITAL. (4). HOTEL

OPERATION 'HUSKY' – the Sicilian Campaign 1943

ALBERGO ITALIANO. (5). SIA GARAGE & M.T. REPAIR SHOP, VIA ROCCO ROMANO. (6). HOUSE, 24 VIA ROCCO ROMANO (HQ, R.A.F.R.). (7). HOUSE, 14 VIA ROCCO ROMANO (Held for R.A.F. Welfare). (8). PIRELLI TYRE STORE. These guards in each case are being maintained during 24hrs of each day until further instructions are received from LT.COL. BOWDERY, HQ, R.A.F.R., or S/LDR GRIFFIN, ADVANCED HEADQUARTERS, D.A.F. The guard was handed over by F/LT FARNSWORTH of 2855 Squadron at 12.00hrs and taken over by the C.O. of 2904 Squadron. 14.00. 6 men were supplied I/C the Flight Sergeant to F/LT.WHITBREAD for special duties at 24, VIA ROCCO ROMANO, H.Q. R.A.F. REGIMENT. 16.00. No.14 M.T.L.R.U. arrived at SITA GARAGE to rendezvous prior to proceeding to FIAT WORKS on the 9th. August.
C.O. & ADJUTANT visited TOWN MAJOR re RATIONS, but no D.I.D. yet established in CATANIA.
Conference of officers to discuss messing, Sanitation, Orders for Guards etc. 10.30. C.O. visited Support and Armoured Flights at CATANIA AIRFIELD. 13.45. LT.COL. BOWDERY, H.Q. R.A.F.R. and WING/CDR.GOULD visited Unit with S/LDR. GRIFFIN. 15.00. C.O. and F/O BAILIE visited Docks area to recce site for guard. Guard on WELFARE HOUSE told to prepare to dismount. 16.00. C.O. visited 2906 Squadron at CATANIA MAIN. 16.30. S/LDR. GRIFFIN requested further guards be placed on the AIRCREW WORKS; and MACHINE SHOPS on the dockside, also om FIAT GARAGE containing vehicles. Request was complied with.
SUB/LT. TOBIASN A.L.O. NAVY HOUSE, visited ADJUTANT re barrack room furniture. 12.00. F/O MANSFIELD visited Unit and further aid was accorded to assist in preparation of H.Q. R.A.F.R. 15.00. F/O JOLIFFE, R.H.Q. D.A.F. visited Unit and requested on behalf of the A.O.A. 1 pl. 10 AC's and one 15cwt.truck for special duties. 17.15. 1 Cpl. 8 AC's and 1 15cwt truck despatched to CAMP COMMANDANT, A.H.Q. D.A.F.17.30. Details of Patrols and Guard Duties forwarded to LT.COL. BOWDERY H.Q. R.A.F.R. REF. 2904S/S1801/1/AIR. 17.35. LT.COL. BOWDERY visited Unit and placed C.O. in charge of Private Villa reserved for H.Q. R.A.F.R.
D/R dispatched to A.H.Q. D.A.F. informing S/LDR. GRIFFIN that Guard on German Aircraft Store had been taken over by the Naval Authorities. (Ref. 2904S/S1800/AIR). 08.30. Telephone line tested

with 86 Area. 86 Area requested to advise this Unit re method of communication with 244 WING. 09.00. CAPT.DRAVERS visited ADJUTANT and requested use of Railway sidings near CATANIS AIRFIELD (Map Ref. 932749) D/R dispatched to A.H.Q. D.A.F. for instructions. (Ref 2904S/S1800/AIR).
Work commenced on clearing rooms and courtyard of S.H.Q. to accommodate Cookhouse and Dining Room. 09.30. C.M.O. & P/O BRODIES visited all guard posts manned by Squadron. 16.30 LT.COL. BOWDERY visited the Unit.
C.O. & ADJUTANT visited Support and Armoured Flights at CATANIA AMIN AERODROME and inspected camp site and billets. 11.00. W/CMDR. GOULD visited Unit. 15.00. S/LDR. GRIFFIN visited Unit re taking over of SITA GARAGE by 3204 Servicing Commando Unit R.A.F.
Court of Inquiry convened for 10.00hrs. on 17th. August, to inquire into the circumstances of an accident involving vehicle WD 91038 on 13th. August. President F/O TURLEY, Member P/O BRODIE. 11.30. Party from 135 A.S.P. with authority of S.E.S.O. D.A.F. collected furniture from warehouse under guard. 15.00. C.O. & ADJUTANT inspected all guard posts and were met by CHIEF ENGINEERING OFFICER and S/LDR. GRIFFIN of D.A.F. during their tour. 16.00. S/LDR GRIFFIN authorised removal of guard from the GRAND HOTEL ITALIA.
ADJUTANT visited CAPT. ALDERCOTTE, 75 C.R.E. re accident involving vehicle WD 91038 on 13th.August. 08.00. "A" Flight took over guard on SITA GARAGE from "B" Flight. 17.30. C.O. attended Regimental conference at H.Q. R.A.F. REGIMENT.

16th – 31st August
2855 (LAA) Sqn – Operational at Lentini West Landing Ground

METEOR. Weather fine. No cloud. Visibility good.
Five airmen of the six previously reported missing on Ship B.B.3. reported at Squadron H.Q. viz: 931635 Cpl. Darling A. 1106249 A/Cpl. Jones R. 1403632 T/Cpl. Edwards D. 1505251 L.A.C. Coplin W. 1535763 L.A.C. Harwood J. Cpl. Darling informed the unit that No.1448715 L.A.C. Saunders N. (Gunner 5) has been left in hospital in N. AFRICA. No official

information regarding this has reached this unit. Report obtained from Cpl. Darling on sinking Ship B.B.3.and subsequent movements of his party until reporting to this Squadron.
METEOR. Weather fine. No cloud. Visibility good.
S/Ldr. H.F. Kinchett resumed command of No.2855 Squadron vice F/Lt. T.J. Tarry on cessation of attachment to "A" Wing R.A.F. Regiment. Auth: R.A.F. Regt. Commander.
METEOR. Weather fine. No cloud. Visibility good.
METEOR. Weather fine. Slight high cloud. Visibility good.
METEOR. Thunderstorms with heavy rain. Cloudy Visibility mainly poor.
METEOR. Cloudy. Rainy periods.
Personnel arrived from No.2859 Squadron for 7-day Hispano A.A. Course to be held at this Squadron commencing 31.8.43. These personnel form pool of re-inforcements for R.A.F. Regiment in Sicily. Authority: R.A.F. Regiment Commander.

2858 (LAA) Sqn – Operational at Palagonia Landing Ground

137847 P/O. Morton, F.H. admitted to No.4 C.C.S.
Practice Shoot held by Squadron. Squadron visited by W/Cdr. Gould, all Gun Sites inspected.
Received General Administrative Instructions for future operations.
Commanding Officer visited W/Cdr. Gould to discuss future operations.
137847 P/O. Morton, F.H. discharged from No.4 C.C.S.
Extensive Squadron training commenced in preparation for future operations. All transport reorganised in preparation.
Four Officers and 40 airmen attended first R.A.F. Regiment Concert at Regiment H.Q.
Squadron Officers attended "At Home" Concert held by No.2855 Squadron.
Commanding Officer visited R.A.F. Regiment H.Q. for the purpose of attending a Conference held by W/Cdr. Gould regarding future operations.
Commanding Officer proceeded to Milazzo to carry out reconnaissance

of Landing strips under construction in the Milazzo area.

Instructions for Operation "Avalanche" received from Adv. H.Q. D.A.F.

2904 (Field) Sqn – Operational at Catania town and aerodrome

C.O. visited TOWM MAJOR re removal of furniture et., from 24 VIA ROCCOROMANO, by former occupants. 11.00. Officials of MINISTRY OF AGRICULTURE afford facilities for removal of office furniture, files, etc. 13.00. F/LT TIFFIN, Entertainments Officer, visited Unit. 15.15. SGT. CLARK, S.I.B. reported having discovered warehouse at 21-22VIA BERNARDO ZANGHI, containing wireless and electrical stores. He requested a guard be placed on premises. ADJUTANT visited premises in company with C.O. No.14 M.T.L.R.U. and arranged for guard to be placed thereon at 17.00 approx. S.E.S.O. R.H.Q., D.A.F. advised accordingly. 16.00. W/CMDR GOULD visited Unit. 18.00. C.O. and ADJUTANT visited German Aircrew Factory and it was considered unnecessary a night guard to be mounted.

Day picket mounted on German A.S.P. 10.45. LT.COL. BOWDERY visited Unit. Court of Inquiry held at S.H.Q. to enquire into the circumstances of an accident involving a 15cwt. Dodge truck WD 91039. 12.00. Message received from civilian that submerged plane down in sea near ACI FRESSA, capable of being salved by use of local fishermen and tackle. 12.30. C.O. visited TOWN MAJOR re requisitioning of 21/29 BERNARDO ZANGHI for R.H.Q. D.A.F. 16.00. S/LDR. GRIFFIN R.H.Q. D.A.F. visited Unit re German A.S.P.at 21/29 BERNADO ZANGHI. 17.00. C.O. & F/O MACMILLAN visited ACI FRESSA and found the plane in 30ft. water. It could not be salvaged with tackle available. 22.00. Operational Order from H.Q. R.A.F.R.:- 2904 Squadron will provide an N.C.O. and 6 men, or one Rifle Section complete, whichever can better be spared, for local defence of personnel moving forward under H.Q. D.A.F. Orders. Personnel to stand by as from 09.00hrs 19th. August, at S.H.Q. for collection. 2. Transport and rations will be provided by H.Q. D.A.F. 3. Acknowledge.

1 Cpl. 6 AC's standing by for special duties with R.H.Q. D.A.F. 13.00. Information received that detachment of 6 AC's and 1 Cpl.

OPERATION 'HUSKY' – the Sicilian Campaign 1943

Despatched to A.H.Q. D.A.F. on 10th. Inst. Have proceeded with advanced party of that Unit to TAOMINA. 14.00. S/LDR. BENSON, Welfare Padre D.A.F. visited F/O BAILIE at S.H.Q. 14.00. The ADJUTANT was admitted to R.A.F. Sick Quarters. 15.00. TOWN MAJOR demanded full particulars of all buildings and rooms occupied by Squadron, together with inventory in use. 17.00. W/CMDR WELLS, DAPM, arrived in CATANIA with F/LT and advanced party of 20 S.P's. 2904 Squadron provided accommodation for the W/CDR. 18.30. F/O WILLIAMSON, 972 Balloon Squadron, called to pick up the party of 6 AC's who had been standing by under H.Q. D.A.F. orders. He decided to stay the night and make contact with a FL/LT HOOD, at Institute of Agriculture, CATANIA, for orders.

Party of 6 men from B Flight left with F/O WILLIAMSON on special duties. No rations taken and no transport provided. 09.00. D.R. arrived from advanced party at TAORMINA and gave address of this party:- VILLA SAN PANCRAZIO, TAORMINA. These men are drawing rations with D.A.F. and carrying out duties of clearing up and guarding premises taken over by D.A.F. 10.00. F/O TYAS, ADJUTANT of 135 A.S.P. called to inspect stores guarded by this Squadron. Informed C.O, that his C.O. S/LDR HOWETT would be at this Headquarters tomorrow, Aug. 20. To inspect and collect stores with necessary authority. S.I.B. called requesting particulars of all equipment at German-Italian Wireless Signals Store. 15.00. LIEUT. THORNDIKE visited Unit and collected stores for A.F.S. from German Park. LT.COL. BOWDERY visited Squadron together with FL/LT WHITBREAD. 18.00. C.O. returned from TAORMINA after inspecting detachment on temporary duty in that town.

F/O PENN visited Unit to collect various stores for 135 A.S.P. from German A.S.P. 11.00. ADJUTANT returned to Squadron. 16.15. F/LT WHITBREAD visited Unit and authorised return of ground floor at 24 VIA ROCCO ROMANO to civilian occupants. Upper floor only to be reserved and guarded for H.Q. R.A.F.R. 16.35. O/C AMGOT NICOLOSA visited ADJUTANT with proprietor of SITA Garage to discuss taking over garage under its former management. ADJUTANT referred him to S/LDR GRIFFIN. R.A.F. 17.30. D.A.P.M. visited Unit. 17.45. F/LT. H.B. ROWLES, O.C. 12. MET. UNIT. A.H.Q. D.A.F. visited Unit and deposited quantity captured enemy Met. Equipment under lock and key

OPERATION 'HUSKY' – the Sicilian Campaign 1943

at SITA Garage.
The C.O., F/LT TURLEY and F/O MACMILLAN proceeded on recce of TAORMINA and to visit and pay detached Section. 08.30. ADJUTANT visited A.H.Q. D.A.F. Accountant Officers. 10.00. W/CMDR WIDEMAN from ALGIERS and Staff Officers visited Unit re taking over SITA Garage as Repair and Maintenance Workshop. 11.00. W/O POTTS 306 M.S.S.U. collected W/T equipment from 21/29 VIA BERNADO ZANGHI. 12.00. R.H.Q. D.A.F., draw refuelling equipment from SITA Garage. 15.30. Squadron Pay Parade.
F/LT. RICHARDSON 324 Wing visited Unit to collect barrack equipment. W/CMDR GOULD "B" Wing H.Q. R.A.F. Regiment visited Unit and requested certain Telephone equipment be made available for collection the following morning. 12.30. F/LT REVILL O.C. 873 A.M.E.S. visited Unit to collect Signals and W/T equipment, om authority of C.S.O. A.H.Q., D.A.F. 16.30. S/LDR. Rogers C of E Padre, D.A.F. visited Unit, a Church Service was arranged for 09.00hrs on 23/8/43. 18.00. Guard on R.A.F. Hospital taken off at request of F/LT FLEMING.
Church Service postponed. 10.00. Dr. PAOLO ANZON permitted to reoccupy flat at 18 VIA LAGO DINICITO. 11.00. Representatives of PIRELLI WORKS requested use of various rooms under supervision of AMGOT. D.A.F. R.H.Q. advised and instructions requested. 15.30. Letter to R.H.Q. D.A.F. requesting instructions regarding taking over SITA Garage by former manager under supervision of AMGOT, to promote civilian bus services. 17.40. Signal from 242 Group, addressed H.Q. N.A.T.A.F. (R) 2904 SQDN. A.D./189 17/8:, Reference loan of 2904 Field Squadron R.A.F.R. please route unit to BORIZZO AERODROME. Notify this H.Q. expected date of arrival. H.Q. R.A.F.R. advised and instructions requested.
F/O TYAS called to collect stationery stores. 10.30. W/CMDR GOULD visited Unit to discuss transport facilities and personnel, and assess necessary shipping required in event for future move. Signal AD/189 17/8 referred to him, and it was decided to get I touch with H.Q. N.A.T.A.F. 10.45. S.E.S.O. W/CMDR STRATFORD JUKES visited Unit to meet manager of SITA Garage.
C.O. and ADJUTANT visited CATANIA AERODROME. 1530. LT.COL. BOWDERY and F/LT WHITBREAD, H.Q. R.A.F.R. visited C.O. 16.00. F/LT ATKINSON

and C.S.O. visited Italian A.S.P. 21/29 VIA BERNARDO ZANGHI. 17.00. Letter DAF/REGT/1/AIR received to effect that no action was to be taken on 242 Group Signal A.D.189 17/8 pending further instructions.
Letter to AHQ, D.A.F. Ref. 701/1/S requesting authority for G.P. 1082/3 TR/RECR, for use as control station at S.H.Q. with A.F.V's. 11.00. 306 M.S.S.U. requisitioned telephone spares from Italian A.S.P. 14.30.O.C. Claims and Hirings, CATANIA visited Unit for details of flats and furniture requisitioned and in use.
Laundry Allowance Pay Parade.10.15. D.A.O.M.C. requested permission to use SITA Garage. 15.00. LT.COL. BOWDERY visited Unit. It was arranged that A Flight proceed to CATANIA AIRFIELD at 15.00hrs on 28th August, for guard and patrol duties on aerodrome. B Flight would take over the guard on SITA Garage and S.H.Q. C Flight would take over guard on German Barrack Stores.
O.C. 3 M.T.L.R.U. visited Unit to obtain authority for 40 double beds for his Unit. 10.00. A Flight moved off to CATANIA MAIN AIRFIELD for Guard and Patrol duties. B Flight took over Guards on SITA Garage and S.H.Q. C Flight took over Guard on German Barrack Stores. 15.00. Party of men from Unit visited H.Q. R.A.F.R. to attend Regimental Concert. 18.15. Officers attended an 'At Home' at 2859 Squadron.
1 15cwt and 1 3tonner loaned to No.4 & "K"
1 15cwt truck from C Flight, and driver,
1 15cwt truck and driver loaned to H.Q. R.A.F.R. for special duties.11.30. TOWN MAJOR visited Unit re requisitioning of German Barrack Stores VIA FRANSESCO CRISPI and possibility of accommodating Docks Operating Coy in premises provisionally. C.O. referred him to S.E.S.O. R.H.Q., D.A.F. 14.00. Signals Training lectures to all Signals Personnel were arranged daily at 14.00hrs, and a weekly programme drawn up.

2906 (Field) Sqn – Moved from Lentini East Landing Ground to Catania Aerodrome (whole of month)

The Squadron was located at Lentini East L.G. Sicily from 31st July to the 4th August 1943. During this period guard was mounted on

OPERATION 'HUSKY' – the Sicilian Campaign 1943

aircraft dispersed around the Landing Ground at night, three armoured cars being placed strategically for immediate action against ground attack., low flying aircraft or airborne troops, the 4th and remaining at H.Q. for W/T contact, and crossing across the runways were guarded throughout the hours of daylight. The Commanding Officer of the Squadron was placed in charge of the Landing Ground, and a Defence Scheme was prepared.

On the morning of the 5th August the Squadron occupied Catania Aerodrome with officers of Technical Intelligence, D.A.F. and Captured Intelligence Technical, U.S.A. N.A.A.F.

The duty assigned to the Squadron was the sealing and guarding of the aerodrome, so as to prevent the removal or destruction of aircraft, equipment, stores, and papers etc. Which would prove of value to the Technical Intelligence branches of the D.A.F. and U.S.A.A.F., also of the R.A.F. generally. The R.A.F. Ensign was hoisted on the morning pf the 6th. August 1943.

Owing to the extent of the duties of the Squadron all personnel with the exception of Cooks and Nursing orderlies had to be employed on guard duties temporarily. Great difficulty was experienced in preventing the removal of serviceable captured aircraft and equipment by personnel of various squadrons of the D.A.F., more especially as the main road traffic had to be diverted through the Aerodrome for a time.

Two captured aircraft (1 Macchi and 1 Fiat C.R.) were removed on the 7th. August 1943 by Officers of 81 and 92 Squadron in direct contravention of definite instructions given immediately prior to their taking off. This occurrence was immediately reported to F/LT ELIINGTON (P.A. to the A.O.C.) who visited the field.

The Intelligence Officers intimated that a great deal of useful information had been obtained from the aerodrome. It was felt however, that had the Squadron been able to arrive earlier, an in full strength a more complete sealing of the aerodrome would have been possible, with consequently greater success in the search for information.

A considerable amount of booby traps, unexploded bombs, and mines were discovered on the aerodrome, and one or two dead bodies had booby traps attached; however, no Squadron personnel were injured by these.

The aerodrome was cleared of mines tec. By 58 Bomb Disposal Unit, R.E., and the runways were made serviceable by 715 Artisan Works Coy. R.E., and 69 C.R.E. (Aerodrome).

On the 19th August, this detachment set out for MESSINA, but could not proceed along the Coast road, and had to make a long detour via Randazzo. The detachment arrived at Messina on 21st. August, and guards were maintained on buildings as requested by Lt. SILVERSTEIN U.S.A.A.F. On the completion of the task, the detachment returned to Catania Airfield on 23rd August on orders of W/Cdr. Gould.

Stores for various Air Stores Parks arrived by air from MAISON BLANCHE on 23rd August, and Squadron personnel off-loaded, also guarded the stores until they were collected by the consignees. On 28th. August No.340 Bomber Group of T.A.F. arrived on the aerodrome to operate there from. The American Flag was flown in place of the R.A.F. Ensign w.e.f. 31st. August.

On 29th. August the Commanding Officer of "D" Coy. 1st Hamps. Regt. Presented an aircrew blade to the Squadron. This blade was off a M.E. 109 which "D" Coy. Shot down over Malta in April 1942. The aircraft had been operating from Catania Aerodrome, and the blade was presented to 2906 Squadron R.A.F., being the first R.A.F. Unit to occupy the same aerodrome in August 1943.

The following detachments from the Squadron were made during the month:-

1 Officer and 49 airmen to No.121 M.U. 31/7/43 to 7/8/43.

1 F/Sgt. And 18 O/R's to Lentini from 1/8/43 to 18/8/43.

1 Cpl. And 6 O/R's to No.121 M.U. (Sub depot) from 2/8/43 to 20/8/43.

1 Sgt. And 150 O/R's to Gerbini L.G. from 4/8/43 to 19/8/43.

1 Officer and Rifle Flight to Gerbini Main from 7/8/43 not yet returns.

1 Officer and 19 O/R's to TAORMINA from 15/8/43 to 23/8/43.

1 Officer and 19 O/R's to Messina from 19/8/43 to 23/8/43.

The administration of the Squadron proved rather difficult during the earlier part of the month, owing to the wide dispersal of attachments, and lack of transport and equipment. Replacements of M.T. were received on 21st August and 22nd August, and Squadron M.T.

was brought up to establishment on the latter date. Demands have been made for the replacement of equipment lost by enemy action.

RECORD OF CASUALTIES.

976154 L.A.C. Petrie R. died of a head wound 8/8/43 following an explosion caused by 274 (N.H) Light A.A. Battery, who were using gelignite to make gun pits about 150 yards away from the aerodrome.

1322663 LAC Ellinor L.V.D. seriously wounded in back, shoulder, and leg during an air raid at No.121 M.U. (No.4 Sub Depot) on might 11/8/43. He was taken to 30 M.F.H., and subsequently evacuated by Air to Tunisia.

F/O C.S. Humberstone and F/O P.L. Briten both received shrapnel wounds in lower limbs during a daylight air attack on 29/8/43, and were removed to 11th. General Hospital.

WELFARE.

Items received from the Welfare Officer D.A.F. during the month included Footballs, Dartboards, Dominoes, and Cards. Two smoking concerts were organised during the month. Swimming parades were held when possible. 4 Officers and 10 airmen attended the concert given by the R.A.F. Regt. Concert party at H.Q. RAF Regt. DAF on 28/8/43. This was the first concert given by the RAF Regt., and two men of this Squadron were in the concert party. The entertainment was enjoyed by all.

OPERATION 'HUSKY' – the Sicilian Campaign 1943

No.2855 Sqn - 'Special Flight' Report

16th. August, 1943.

"SPECIAL FLIGHT" COMMANDER'S REPORT ON CATANIA GUARD.

In accordance with Eight Army Instructions, received at 16.00 hours on 5th. August, 1943, I proceeded with a special flight to CATANIA (in convoy with other reconnaissance units detailed in the "Golden List" published by the Eight Army on 4th. August, 1943) leaving my flight location at 20.00 hours.

Flight H.Q. was established at the FIAT WORKS and a guard was posted there, at the HOTEL ALBERGA ITALIANO and at the SITA works in VIA ROCCO ROMANO; all these building having been requisitioned by D.A.F.

At 08.00 hours on 6th. August, 1943 I was ordered by S/Ldr. Griffen to supply a guard for CATANIA HOSPITAL, which was to be used as a hospital by Allied Forces. This was done at 08.15 hours.

At 09.00 hours I received an order for a guard to be posted at a storehouse containing barrack furniture at VIA FRANCESCO CRISPI. This was done at 09.20 hours.

At 09.30 hours I moved Flight H.Q. to the SITA garage where better cooking facilities and running water were available. Guards were transported to the SITA garage to meals from this time onwards, in two relays.

At 10.00 hours guards were posted in VIA ROCCOROMANO at three buildings which had been requisitioned on orders from L/Col. Bowdery M.C. Commanding R.A.F. Regiment, as H.Q. These buildings had already been broken open and were in considerable disorder. This fact was reported to the Town Major when the building s were formally registered with him.

At 10.15 hours a Sergeant of the Italian Army surrendered to Cpl. Medway ay the SITA works. He was placed under guard, after being searched for weapons, and handed over to 86 Area.

At 12.00 hours I was visited by the Squadron Commander.

At 14.00 hours S/Ldr. Griffin ordered me to post a continuous guard on the PIRELLI works and store. As my force was already totally committed, I sent an armoured car with crew to take over the building at 14.20 hours.

At 19.15 hours I received orders from Squadron Commander to hand over all guards to No. 2904 Squadron when they arrived.

At 12.00 hours on 8th, August, 1943 the handing over was completed.

At 13.00 hours I proceeded from CATANIA for Squadron H.Q.

At 14.00 hours arrived at Squadron H.Q.

Flight Lieutenant, Commanding,

"Special Flight" 2855 Sqdn.

OPERATION 'HUSKY' – the Sicilian Campaign 1943

No.2855 Sqn Action Report - 11th August 1943

ACTION REPORT.

For 24 hours ending 06.30 hours on 12th. August, 1943.

1. PLACE.   LENTINI WEST LANDING GROUND.
2. TIME.   22.40 hours 11.8.43.
3. METEOR.   Bright moonlight.
4. NATURE OF ATTACK.   Dive bombing. Low level bombing.
5. DIRECTION OF ATTACK. Mainly S.W. to N.E. but during engagement attacks were delivered from all directions.
6. ESTIMATED NUMBER OF AIRCRAFT.   20.
7. ESTIMATED HEIGHT OF AIRCRAFT.   Around 1,000 feet.
8. ILLUNINANTS USED.   Chandelier flares, concentration flare. Red and green signal flares.
9. GUNS IN ACTION. All 16 guns.
10.   Ammunition expended. 857 rounds 20m.m
11.   NUMBER OF AIRCRAFT CLAIMED AS DAMAGED.   One.
    a. Claimed by No.5 and No.11 Guns.
    b. Observation in support of claim: Report by F/Lt. Farnworth (attached)
12.   NUMBER OF AIRCRAFT CLAIMED AS SHOT DOWN.   Nil.
13.   GUNS OUT OF ACTION.
    a. No.13 Gun out of action from 13.15 hours to 06.00 hours.
    b. Reason – Defective firing pin.
    c. Gun now serviceable.
14.   SQUADRON EQUIPMENT DAMAGED.
    2 Tented G.S.
    3 Bivouacs.
    Sundry personal kits.
    NAAFI stores (Value to be determined)
    6 Blankets. (Loaned to 1st. aid parties)
15.   DAMAGETO AIRFIELD IN SQUADRON AREA.
    Sundry craters on both sides of landing ground and on runway.
16.   CASUALTIES

(a) Killed.	(b). Wounded.	(c) Missing.
Nil.	No. 1355517 Cpl. Rogerson W.	Nil.
	No. 1809081 A.C.1. Newman G.	

17.   REMARKS.
18.   After the raid fires were still burning on the airfield in the vicinity of operations. Personnel were formed into firefighting parties and assisted ground crews.

Flight Lieutenant, Commanding,

No. 2855 Squadron, R.A.F. Rgt.

"B" Wing - AUGUST 1943

Overview

Arriving at the new landing ground at Agnone, 2856 L.A.A. Squadron soon pitched its tents and had its 16 Hispano cannons positioned. Working with the Army A.A. Units, who provided Bofor, as well as heavy gun support, the defence A.A. barrage was agreed. The squadron loaned other Hispano cannon and cooking equipment from other Regiment units and was soon operationally effective.

Moving from the island of Gozo, 2862 L.A.A. Squadron arrived at Agnone landing ground to work alongside 2856 Squadron. It's 18 Hispano cannons were soon positioned, however the units commanding officer was not happy with the opening fire orders which used 'Umbrella' barrage or 'Set Direction' manoeuvres, which from his experience in North Africa, rendered the Hispanos ineffective.

Both squadrons where in action on the night of the 11th August air raid, where anti-personnel bombs were dropped on the landing ground. Although both squadrons suffered casualties as a result of the raid, 2862 L.A.A. Squadron lost 4 airmen that night.

Map showing the 'B' Wing Units at the end of August 1943

(Source: Author Adapted http://d-maps.com/m/europa/italia/sicile/sicile15.gif)

On arriving at the Scordia landing ground, 2857 L.A.A. Squadron found the routine of defence running smoothly. However, around 10% of the unit's establishment was now sick in hospital and on the 12th August, the squadron received the news of its first fatality to cerebral malaria.

It didn't take 2859 L.A.A. Squadron long to settle down at San Francesco landing ground, and the unit was able to loan anti-aircraft cannons, to replace the equipment it had lost in the shipping air raid. It was also decided to set up a Hispano Gunnery School at the landing ground, where all units would participate in the short courses on offer.

Lentini East landing ground, under the protection of 2925 L.A.A. Squadron suffered tremendously from the heavy enemy air raid on 11th August. Direct hits on the landing ground killed 11 airmen, 8 airmen (6 from 'A' Flight alone), and 3 originally injured, later died of their wounds. Lessons learnt from the raid were immediately actioned, moving the flights away from the dispersal areas and into areas on the side of the landing grounds, which would give them complete coverage against low flying aircraft.

A number of key points were also raised by the commander of 2862 L.A.A. Squadron, around the need for more tracer rounds, more ammunition kept at gun posts, the standardisation of the number of loaded magazines at day and night and the reinforcement of slit trenches at the gun post areas.

On the other side of the island, 2864 L.A.A. Squadron landed off Palermo and proceeded to the main aerodrome, which was under American control. It soon got into the defensive routine, including the repairing of the perimeter fencing and providing guard at the main entrance. On the 29th August, the squadron undertook a secret mission to hide an Italian aircraft and its crew, which would land on the aerodrome that evening, transporting important Italian dignitaries.

With the surrender of the island, the latter part of the month was taken up with training programmes and servicing of vehicles and equipment for the next campaign. For the men, some time for rest and recuperation, with the occasional concert and bathing sessions.

OPERATION 'HUSKY' – the Sicilian Campaign 1943

Operational Diaries

1st – 15th August
2856 (LAA) Sqn – Operational at Agnone Landing Ground

After an early breakfast, the 2nd in Command, F/LT. PEATTIE left with 14 drivers to collect the Units vehicles which were to be landed to-day from G.G.3, H.M.T. EMPIRE NEWTON. The vehicles were to be landed at 33 BEACH UNIT – "ACID BEACH", about 10 miles South of SYRACUSA. This news had been eagerly awaited by all ranks as the SQUADRON can now perform its intended operational role.
Visit from W/C. GOULD, Commanding "B" WING H.Q., who departed with COMMANDING OFFICER to approve his reconnaissance of AGNONE LANDING GROUND. The COMMANDING OFFCIER took a sketch map showing selected FLIGHT AREAS and on returning reported that they were approved. During the morning a Medical Officer visited the Unit and gave useful advise on sanitation. Following this A/CDR. ATCHERLY came and enquired when we were moving, explaining in brief the A.A. DEFENCE SCHEME for the LANDING GROUND.
The COMMANDING OFFICER departed with the EQUIPMENT SERGEANT in search of MOSIQUITO NETS and sanitary equipment – essential items which had been overlooked by the authorities in the UNITED KINGDOM.
Message from the 2nd in Command that 9 vehicles were off-loaded and had proceeded to AGNONE, the remaining vehicles not being expected ashore until to-morrow.
20 airman from "C" Flight left for AGNONE to act as unloading party. Patrols and Listening Posts inspected and given their orders. During the evening orders were issued for the movement of the SQUADRON the following morning.
The COMMANDING OFFICER left for AGNONE LANDING GROUND as the remainder of the SQUADRON was to move during the morning, vehicles coming to transport the FLIGHTS as soon as stores were unloaded.
2 vehicles arrived to convey HEADQUARTERS FLIGHT and "B" FLIGHT to AGNONE. During the morning the remaining FLIGHTS were transported to AGNONE and immediately went to their selected areas and erected guns. 16 guns were ready for action by 15.00hrs. Tents were pitched and all FLIGHTS established in their areas.
The remaining vehicles which had been off-loaded during the morning

OPERATION 'HUSKY' – the Sicilian Campaign 1943

arrived and were immediately unloaded.
329 WING arrived consisting of 5 SQUADRONS of KITTYHAWKS – The AIRFIELD CONSTRUCTION COY having prepared 2 excellent landing strips. AGNONE AREA is low lying by the sea and during the rainy season must be a marshy area. Bathing facilities are excellent, but mosquitos abound in millions and we are informed that this is a bad area for them on the ISLAND. A cool breeze from the sea makes the heat less noticeable.
W/O. O'REILY attended a conference for REGIMENT W/O's at REGIMENT HEADQUARTERS – SCORDIA. By dusk all sections of the SQUADRON were functioning and equipment was stored, the chief difficulty having been the intermittent arrival of the vehicles from the off-loading beach.
SQUADRON COMMANDERS conference attended by all SQUADRON OFFICERS, when signals for opening fire and the proposed A.A. BARRAGE systems were explained. This unit has a definite role to fulfil in co-operation with the ARMY A.A. UNITS. The LANDING GROUND seems to be protected from the A.A. point of view.
The ADJUTANT attended a conference at R.A.F. REGIMENT HEADQUARTERS, SCORDIA. As a result of this it became more evident than ever that the amount of paper work required would increase – this is not what the unit expected, as it left the UNITED KINGDOM under the impression that matters essentially operational would be uppermost in everyones minds.
COMMANDING OFFICER attended a conference with the STATION COMMANDER and A.A. COMMANDER and new areas allotted to the FLIGHTS on the sand dunes facing the sea. During the morning a new map was made showing these areas. For day firing the SQUADRON is responsible for giving the warning of all low flying hostile aircraft approaching from the sea. The remainder of the morning and afternoon was spent by the FLIGHTS in moving to their new areas – selecting gun positions and H.Q's.
COMMANDING OFFICER and ADJUTANT toured FLIGHT AREAS – the guns were in position with excellent background and would not be visible until opening fire. All guns manned 24hrs. DAY and NIGHT. – no activity.
FLIGHT AREAS were completed and UNIT stores checked. A telephone was installed by the ARMY SIGNALS UNIT giving communications with 329

OPERATION 'HUSKY' – the Sicilian Campaign 1943

WING.
SQUADRON LEADER VIDLER, OFFICER COMMANDING 2859 SQUADRON, visited the unit. 3- 20m.m. Hispanos were loaned to his unit together with some cooking equipment, as part of his equipment had been lost in transit. 3 vehicles loaned to 2906 SQUADRON.
COMMANDING OFFICER informed all FLIGHT COMMANDERS of the composition of the A.A. Defence of the landing ground. Units were from the 73rd. A.A. BRIGADE - 36 Bofor Guns of 61 LAA BATTERY and 215 LAA BATTERY and 2 heavy BATTERIES Nos. 336 and 161. FLIGHT bathing parades commenced during the morning and afternoon and were instituted as a part of the normal routine.
"A" FLIGHT reported to Landing Craft approaching the beach close inshore. These were unidentified and all FLIGHTS were standing to. Eventually it was established that they were our craft, but the alarm had its use as it showed up the difficulties of communicating between the FLIGHTS and SQUADRON HEADQUARTERS.
COMMANDING OFFICER visited the STATION COMMANDER and arranged a practice shoot for the following day. All W/T equipment was tested and 6,000 rounds reserve of 20 m.m. ammunition was obtained. The COMMANDING OFFICER visited SYRACUSA to find out the location of the Unit's sick and injured personnel. All seem to be evacuated to the Main Land - sick personnel only being kept on the ISLAND for 48 hrs unless too ill to be moved.
After contacting all A.A. BATTERIES on the Landing Ground, the FLIGHTS held a practice shoot. Guns were fired into the sea with excellent results. There were no stoppages and all personnel fired with confidence, each member of "A" and "B" FLIGHT gun crews firing off a magazine. The guns put up a barrage which would have given any low flying approaching hostile aircraft a warm reception. News received that 2862 SQUADRON were moving to AGNONE on 9th August, 1943 and the COMMANDING OFFICER was to recce positions for them. W/T frequency of 8.9m/cs. Was allotted to this unit as it does not interfere with that used by flying squadrons.
A practice shoot was held by the BOFORS - we had not received any warning that this was to take place. 1 Sergeant, 3 Corporals and 6 O.R's were detached to 2859 SQUADRON for a short course on the HISPANO at SAN FRANCESCO L.G. This unit

OPERATION 'HUSKY' – the Sicilian Campaign 1943

also provided an instructor. The reason for these courses is a mystery as this unit was particularly well trained before leaving the UNITED KINGDOM. As a result the full number of guns could not be manned.
F/LT. PEATTIE proceeded to SYRACUSA to ascertain where 2862 SQUADRON were to land and if they would need vehicles to move them. They were to take up positions inside the ring of BOFORS guns near to the runways, approximately in this unit's first positions.
F/LT. PEATTIE returned from SYRACUSA and AUGUSTA with a report that no trace could be found of 2862 SQUADRON, having arranged for "B" WING, R.A.F. REGIMENT to be informed as soon as they landed. During the afternoon further W/T tests were made. "C" FLIGHT had perfect reception, but "A" FLIGHT were at first unable to contact HEADQUARTERS. The 2 vehicles loaned to 2906 SQUADRON returned to this unit. 2862 SQUADRON, complete with transport arrived unexpectedly during the evening.
Enemy aircraft raided AUGUSTA and CATANIA and heavy barrages were put up. There was activity to the NORTH and SOUTH of the Landing Ground but our guns did not open fire. More raids are to be expected as the moon period has began.
2862 SQUADRON settled in, making their HEADQUARTERS in the far corner of our field. This unit provided them with maps of the area and gave them all possible help. During the "C" FLIGHT gun crews had a Hight Judging Test and Sighting practice through the co-operation of No.3 SQUADORN'S aircraft.
COMMANDING OFFICER prepared a tracing of A.A. positions and completed the DEFENCE SCHEME for AGNONE LANDING GROUND. Sickness and courses have caused "A" FLIGHT to man 5 guns only – this unit has yet to suffer cases of Malaria although it was learned that 30 cases had occurred in a Heavy A.A. unit dur to 10 days shortage of Mepacrine.
A heavy and accurate raid commenced, many flares, incendiaries and Anti-personnel bombs were dropped on the Landing Ground. The Hispanos opened on signal from the Master Gun and did well. "B" FLIGHT suffered 3 casualties 1318789 Lac. VINCENT, S. 1633913 Ac1. FINDER, R., and 1459451 Lac. WICKENS, M. J. all shrapnel injuries. All these airmen were members of Corporal CHURCHMAN gun crew and he

showed fine example by keeping his gun firing for which action a recommendation for an Honour was submitted. The raid ended at 23.20hrs. As a result of the raid the following points arise – (i) More tracer ammunition required and more ammunition on the gun posts themselves (ii) 6 Magazines loaded for night time and 3 by day. (iii) Slit trenches require some wooden protection.

The COMMANDING OFFICER, ADJUTANT and F/O. RADWAY-MILLS went to 329 WING HOSPITAL where this unit provided 60 blankets and a water tender, the SENIOR MEDICAL OFFICER being grateful for the assistance. 2862 SQUADRON suffered 4 dead and 3 injured.

The general comment was that the airmen were very pleased that they were able to hit back and glad to have a go. There was an excellent spirit all round. Courses now seem to be farcical.

The AIRFIELD was operational, no further casualties have come to light and everyone has settled down to normal routine. This unit had expended 3,000 rounds of ammunition the previous night. Col. BOWDERY and W/C. GOULD paid a visit during the morning. Airmen returned from the Hispano Courses to-day and seem to have enjoyed it. FLIGHTS put covers over slit trenches for protection against Anti-personnel bombs and decided to put sand bags round the guns except for the frontal ground to ground arcs. Further supplies of ammunition were obtained.

999500 Lac. FINDLAY N.A. of "B" FLIGHT received a gun shot wound in the foot whilst cleaning his rifle. A Court of Enquiry was ordered F/LT.G.R. MILLS being the investigating officer.

The STATION COMMANDER ordered that Hispanos should not open fire at night except on seen targets. 1266471 Lac. WILSON, L. returned from 97 GENERAL HOSPITAL, TUNIS, landed at LE. CATA with AMERICANS and had to hike back to AGNONE.

2862 (LAA) Sqn – Move from the island of Gozo, operational at Agnone Landing Ground

Instructions received to use the Squadron for loading petrol etc. on the docks from the aerodrome
Forty Squadron personnel employed on cleaning up the aerodrome and moving stores to the docks.
Squadron-Leader Sheil to Valetta on Temporary Duty.

OPERATION 'HUSKY' – the Sicilian Campaign 1943

Instruction received that 2862 L.A.A. Squadron was to give their maximum effort in cleaning up the aerodrome. Loading and unloading Petrol, Bombs and Ammunition on L.C.T.'s for Malta.
Squadron Leader Sheil returned to unit from Valette.
F/Lt. Jones discharged from hospital and returned to Unit.
Personnel used on Aerodrome clearance work.
Air Raid warning at 12.20hrs. No attack developed.
Ten days' Battle Rations drawn.
Verbal message received that the Squadron was to embark that day for Malta by LCI. And L.S.T. Five Officers and 133 O.R.s embarked at 16.30hrs, by L.C.I. for Malta, arriving 19.00hrs and proceeding to Luga Aerodrome to await further instructions. All personnel were accommodated there.
The C.O. and Adjutant, together with 22 O.R.s, including 13 drivers, 13 – 3 ton lorries and 1 Jeep embarked at 12.20hrs for Malta on L.S.T., arriving 17.00hrs that day.
Orders were given to remain on board. Embarked for Sicily – No.1 Party by L.C.I. and No.2 – that is, the party left on board the L.S.T. -by the same vessel. 1 Officer (F/O Chanin) left in Victoria Hospital, Gozo, also 6 O.R.s left in the 39th General Hospital. The journey was without incident.
Destination Syracuse was changed en route to Port Augusta, arriving 12.00hrs. The Squadron proceeded to disembark, during which period without warning the harbour was attacked by 6 Italian aircraft. 1 bomb dropped, neither damage nor casualties sustained. The Squadron proceeded to No.2 Assembly Area Port, Augusta, whilst the Adjutant contacted the Embarkation Officer for further instructions. At 17.00hrs the Squadron left for Agnone, some 25 miles N.E. of this area, arriving at 20.00hrs with the exception of 3 vehicles – two of which eventually came in, having developed trouble en route. Temporary camp erected for the night.
Rations sent out to the lorry broken down outside Carlentini. Permanent Camp prepared and Guns sighted – only 18 Hispanos. The Commanding Officer visited the Station Commander, G/Cpt. Darwen and Major Andrews A.A.D.C. W/Cdr. Gould visited the camp and was seen by the C.O. He informed the Commanding Officer that Lieut. Colonel C.D. Bowdery was i/c R.A.F.R. and was trying to form a

OPERATION 'HUSKY' – the Sicilian Campaign 1943

R.A.F.R. Group to consist of two wings 'A' & 'B'; we were to come under 'B' Wing
The Commanding Officer and Adjutant went to the A.H.Q., D.A.F. and opened an Imprest Account in the Adjutant's name, also drawing £400. A visit was paid to 322 Wing, R.A.F.R., H.Q., to see W/Cdr. Gould.
Orders were given re opening of fire "Day and Night".   The Commanding Officer did not like the Orders re opening fire at night time, which consisted of either "Umbrella Barrage" or "Set Direction". From experience gained in the N.W.A. Campaign, with 20 m.m. Hispanos we found it paid better to hold fire until a good target was presented, especially as we had no tracer ammunition.   At about 22.50hrs, a severe raid developed on the Airfield, all guns opened fire as ordered. The first stick of bombs fell in and around 'B; Flight who were in Action on the North end of the North South runway. The following were killed outright:-   Sgt. Ousten, LAC. Smith (409), LAC. Witts. LAC. Ankell died of wounds the following day. 10 other N.C.O.s and Airmen were wounded including Cpl. Manion who was detained in hospital. Three lorries were also damaged.   All Officers were at their posts as soon as possible, and a fine spirit was shown by all N.C.O.s and airmen throughout the raid. Special mention must be made to Cpl. Mirkin, Cpl. Lang, Cpl. Kerr, LAC. Hudson, LAC. Waddle, LAC. Hennessy.   CPL. MIRKIN -During a very heavy raid on Agnone aerodrome on the night of 11th August, 1943, this airman showed great courage and devotion to duty.   In the first stages of the raid this Corporal's Section was hit by a large number of A.P. Bombs killing four men and wounding eleven. He himself was hit in several places, but in spite of this immediately crossed the aerodrome on foot to obtain assistance from the M.O., whom he guided back to the stricken section. He had his most serious wound dressed by the M.O. and dressed the rest of his wounds himself.   H.E. and A.P. Bombs were being dropped in large numbers during the whole of this time.   CPL. KERR. - During a very heavy raid on Agnone aerodrome on the night of 11th August, 1943, this airman showed great courage and

devotion to duty.

In the first stages of the raid a Section of this airman's Flight was hit by A.P. bombs, killing four and wounding eleven men. He immediately drove his three ton lorry about 200 yards to the stricken Section and then drove across the aerodrome, whilst a large number of H.E. and A.P. bombs were falling to fetch assistance from H.Q.

CPL. LANG. - During a very heavy raid on Agnone aerodrome on the night of 11th August, 1943, this airman showed great courage and devotion to duty.

At the height of the raid he took a three ton lorry on to the aerodrome, in order to pick up casualties, and convey them to hospital. Whilst driving he ran great risk from the large number of H.E. and A.P. bombs being dropped at the time.

LAC. Hudson, LAC. Waddle and LAC. Hennessy worked continually during the raid and helped and assisted in every way possible.

At 12.15hrs Sgt. Ouston, LAC. Smith (409), LAC. Witts were buried at Agnone.

All officers attended the funeral.

At 15.30hrs LAC. Arkell was buried at Agnone. F/O. B.W. Short and F/O W. Odgers attended.

All action was taken on Signals, reports and kit, etc.

Four Crosses were made and placed on the graves.

F/O Steen admitted to 329 Wing hospital.

Short Course of Instruction was started in the Flights on the Hispano.

The Commanding Officer attended Senior Officers conference of R.A.F.R. The question of the condition of the Squadron Transport was raised.

2857 (LAA) Sqn – Operational at Scordia Landing Ground

Squadron moved to Scordia airfield. No.66 Fighter bomber Squadron, Americans in command. Guns sighted and manned. Much better location for Squadron.

Squadron settled and working comfortably. One or two cases of sand fly.

OPERATION 'HUSKY' – the Sicilian Campaign 1943

Remainder of lorries arrived, unpacked and stores distributed.
Remainder of guns sighted and manned. Heat beginning to affect Airmen.
H.Q. take over farmhouse, which apparently had not long been vacated by the Italians, quantities of ammunition and gun parts left behind by the enemy.
Routine work running smoothly. Transport being thoroughly overhauled ready for the next move which should not be very long.
All are beginning to work in close contact with American Squadrons. Mosquitos seem to be quite rare in the particular region. A smaller number of men are reporting sick due I think to eating fruit.
No more reported cases of sickness. Have laid down that all fruit must be washed in permanganate of Potash. Expecting to move to Gebini Airfield any day.
Went to Catania, town very badly Blitzed, inhabitants beginning to return in quite large numbers. Enemy aircraft appear to be attacking the port of Augusta in some strength.
Administration running smoothly despite the fact of an ever increasing flow of correspondence between Squadrons and R.A.F. Regiment Headquarters.
Numbers of men now in hospital total 12. This fact is causing us some concern, because at the moment we have no reserves to draw from.
Enemy aircraft bombed adjacent Airfields at about 22.00hrs. Some damages and casualties reported. This Squadron has neither damage or casualties to report. C.O. went to Syrcuse to try and find our men who had been evacuated from 4. C.C.S. to Syracuse only to discover that with the exception of one man all had been evacuated to North Africa.
Signal received from 25 M.F.H. confirming is of the death of 1652810 Lac Noble on the 12th August, 1943 at 11.25hrs cause of death Cerebral Malaria. 10% of Squadron have now been admitted to hospital. Position is causing us grave concern, and every effort has and is being made to impress upon the personnel the absolute necessity to sterilizing their eating and cooking utensils and

instructions have been definitely laid down that only sterilized water is to be used.
Although it is almost on full moon, there has not yet been any Blitz on this Advanced landing Ground.
Extremely hot. Two airmen returned from Sick Quarters.

2859 (LAA) Sqn – Operational at San Francesco Landing Ground

Squadron have settled down in new location, all guns manned and ready for action. An unfortunate accident occurred this afternoon when LAC. HARWOOD picked up an enemy detonator which exploded in his hand causing laceration of fingers on both hands. He was admitted to No.30. M.F.H.
Normal Squadron routine. Nothing to report.
Normal Squadron routine. Nothing to report.
Normal Squadron routine. Nothing to report. Defence scheme has been laid out for SAN FRANCESCO L.G.
Owing to the loss in transit of certain Squadron Equipment, it has been necessary to take on loan a number of 20mm. Hispano Cannons in order that the Squadron may become fully operational. 3 Hispanos have been received on loan from No. 2857 A.A. Squadron R.A.F.R., today.
4 Hispano Cannons have been received on loan from No. 2856 A.A. Squadron, R.A.F.R., and 3. German Flak Guns from No. 2925 A.A. Squadron. LAC. HESLING was admitted to Hospital today and his case has been diagnosed as Malaria. It has been decided to run a 20mm. Cannon Course for all local Regiment Squadrons in the district and it has been necessary to obtain a number of extra guns. 3 20mm. Hispano Cannons have been received on loan from No. 2855 A.A. Squadron, R.A.F.R. for this course, today.
Normal Squadron Routine. The Squadron Concert Party which has been formed by the Entertainment Officer, F/Lt. SCOTT gave it's first concert this evening and was enjoyed by all.
1. 20mm. Hispano Cannon was received on loan from No.2856 Squadron

today. (For A.A. Course) A Church of England Service was held on the Squadron site at 17.00 hrs,
The 20mm. Cannon Course commenced today and the School consisted of 62 Airmen made up of as follows:- 11 - 2859 Sqdn., 10-2925 Sqdn.,10-2856 Sqdn., 10 - 2855 Sqdn., 10 - 2858 Sqdn., and 11 -2857 Sqdn. F/Lt. VAUGHAN is chief instructor on the course.
Hispano Cannon Course in progress. 1. 20mm. Cannon received on loan from 2925 Sqdn.
Normal Squadron Operational Routine. A Roman Catholic service was held at 09.30hrs. At 23.20hrs the Airfields within close proximity to this one were attacked by enemy aircraft, although no direct attack was made on SAN FRANCESCO L.G. Duration of attack 35 minutes. This was the Squadron's first action, and all personnel expressed satisfaction at being able to get to grips with the enemy.
Normal Squadron Operational Routine. No.1. 20mm. Hispano Cannon course completed.
Normal Squadron Operational Routine.
Normal Squadron Operational Routine. The Squadron Concert Party gave its second concert in the evening, and enjoyed by a large audience.
Normal Squadron Operational Routine. A Church of England Service was held on the Squadron site at 17.00hrs.

2925 (LAA) Sqn – Operational at Lentini East Landing Ground

The main event during this month was a "blitz" on LENTINI EAST L.G. on 11th August. This was the first time that the Unit had been in action against a concentrated attack on the L.G. they were defending. The attacks at PANCHINO were desultory and over a wide area, no bombs were actually dropped, or aimed, at the L.G. itself and the guns only opened fire when enemy aircraft passed over the L.G. The main lesson learned from the attack on the 11th., was that the guns should not be sited on the edge of the runways and in dispersal areas where they are likely to be neutralised by bombing. Guns should be sited away from the target so as to cover approaches.

OPERATION 'HUSKY' – the Sicilian Campaign 1943

Further, with the present non-self-destructing ammunition, Hispano should not open fire unless they can see the target and have a reasonable chance of hitting it.

1 Sergeant 3 Corporals and 6 AC's attached to 2859 Squadron for special A.A. Course.

During the night at approximately 23.00hrs the L.G's at LENTINI (East and West), SAN FRANCESCO and SCORDIA were attacked by a large force of enemy aircraft. The attacks on LENTINI EAST lasted for about an hour and during this time several sticks of H.E. were dropped across the runways and dispersal areas and a large number of "crackerjack" anti-personnel bombs were scattered over the L.G., the dispersal areas and the surrounding country. Six men of 'A' Flight, 1272583, CPL. CAWLEY, 1114987, CPL. CORBISHLEY, 652775 L.A.C. TULLY, 1450065, L.A.C. HUMPHRIES, 1484947, L.A.C. PAUL, 1502683, LAC COE were killed by direct hits on their posts by H.E. Bombs. 1391605, L.A.C. HAYDEN, 1272522 L.A.C. RUNDLE, 1315638, L.A.C. WHALEY were seriously injured. One man of 'B' Flight 1350101 L.A.C. WILSEA was killed by blast from H.E. Bombs. There were no casualties in 'C' Flight but one vehicle was burned out and all suffered damage from shrapnel.

The A.A. barrage was very weak, there being only a few Bofor Guns to support the Hispanos and no heavy A.A. So far as in known, no enemy aircraft were brought down by A.A. fire. Several Hispanos were u/s after firing a few rounds, but the German "flak" guns gave a good account of themselves? Their rate of fire is slower but the ammunition is self-destructive and the mounting is much superior to the Hispano.

1358497, Cpl. DORSETT, G. was in charge of the post which had a "near miss" from a heavy bomb. Though severely shaken he continued to operate his gun until it became u/s. He has been recommended for the M.M.

1473164, L.A.C. WOOLMER and 1172208, L.A.C. YOUNG showed great courage and devotion to duty by going to the assistance of the wounded despite the fact that the Flight ammunition dump had been set on fire and the ammunition was exploding. These airmen have been recommended for "Mention in Despatches".

'A' Flight's position being untenable due to exploding ammunition and all the guns being u/s, the Flight was moved to Squadron Headquarters for the night.

The Flights were-sited during the day. 'A' Flight, having insufficient men to operate as a Flight, was absorbed in 'B' and 'C' Flights.
'B' Flight moved to the crest of the hill on the West side of the L.G., 'C' Flight to the hill on the south side. Both positions enable the guns to give a complete cover against low flying attacks from any quarter.
M.T. spent the days servicing vehicles prior to moving away from the aircraft dispersal areas.
LAC. HAYDEN and LAC. WHALEY died in 30 M.F.H.
The funeral of all killed was held at 17.00hrs, Officers and all men of "A" Flight attended.
Personnel returned from Special A.A. course at 2859 Squadron.

F/O. WALTON went to No.4 C.C.S. to see LAC. RUNDLE, one of 'A' Flights injured in the raid and was informed that the airman had died and had been buried on 13th August, 1943. This Unit had not been informed and the authorities did not appear to know that the airman did belong to this Unit. His personal effects had been sent to P.M.O., C.M.F.

2864 (LAA) Sqn – From Tunis, disembarked for Palermo Aerodrome

Information received from Transport Officer No.67 E.U. that this Unit was to proceed to Tunis early tomorrow. Transport would be provided at 15.00hrs for loading and routing instructions would be given later.

An R.A.S.C. convoy consisting of 38 old and unreliable vehicles, several unserviceable, reported to this Unit. All stores and equipment loaded.

Transport Officer No.67 E.U. visited O.C. with Routing Instructions.

Convoy left for Tunis.
O.C. and 2nd i/c went ahead and visited O.C. R.A.F. Movement Control Tunis who stated that there was no available shipping for immediate move to Palermo and this Unit would have to wait pro tem at staging

OPERATION 'HUSKY' – the Sicilian Campaign 1943

area at Arizona – Map. Ref. TUNISIA 1/200000, Sheet 3, 0664. O.C. arranged with Embarkation Officer Tunis that Squadron equipment and stores should be immediately unloaded at the docks at La Goulette (Map. Ref. Tunisia 1/200000 Sheet 6 0858), except essential camp equipment, ready for shipment. This arrangement was carried into effect and Squadron pitched camp at Arizona.
No occurrence of importance.
Visited by S/Ldr Symons, R.A.F. Regiment Staff Officer, 242 Group, who had flown from Palermo to ascertain the reason for delay in arrival of this Unit. Arrangements made to notify him by Air Courier of probable dates of sailing and arrival.
No occurrence of importance.
Col. M. Salmon, M.C., Commander R.A.F. Regiment, N.A.A.F. visited this Unit at Arizona. Projected move to Palermo discussed and also general organisation and administration of Squadron.
Orders received from Embarkation Officer Tunis to load equipment on to L.S.T. No. 338 today and that 100 personnel would sail on this ship, and must be ready to embark at 09.00hrs tomorrow. All vehicles to be loaded on L.S.T. No. 346 at 09.30hrs tomorrow and remainder of personnel to embark at that time. Equipment loaded on L.S.T. No. 338 today and camp stuck.
Visit by Col. M. Salmon, M.C., who advised that he had transferred 3 Motor Cycles to this Unit from other Squadrons. These were delivered prior to his departure.
Squadron H.Q. and Nos.1 and 3 Flights left staging area and embarked on L.S.T. No.338 at La Goulette.
Col. M. Salmon, M.C., visited O.C. L.S.T. 338 and handed to him a complete set of maps of Sicily.
No.2 Flight commanded by F/O. Wright embarked with all Squadron vehicles in L.S.T. 346.
L.S.T's Nos. 338 and 346 remained in dock at La Goulette.
Both L.S.T's set sail in convoy.
Approx. Convoy arrived off Palermo.
Approx. L.S.T's docked. Unloading of Unit equipment delayed several hours pending unloading of other cargo.
O.C. proceeded to Palermo aerodrome, Map Ref. ITALY 1/250000 Sheet

OPERATION 'HUSKY' – the Sicilian Campaign 1943

49 3746 and contacted S/Ldr Symons at 1st A.D.W. who arranged with an American unit for transport to be sent to the docks for unloading, and indicated dispersal area allotted to this Unit.

16th – 31st August
2856 (LAA) Sqn – Operational at Agnone Landing Ground

FLIGHTS held practice shoot firing guns out to sea. This unit had its first case of Malaria.
A further vehicle loaned to 2906 SQUADRON COMMANDING OFFICER visited W/C. GOULD at 322 WING HEADQUARTERS and learned that operations were being planned.
W/C. GOULD visited SQUADRON and informed COMMANDING OFFICER that this unit had been selected for an operation. Everything to be on top line – airmen – vehicles – guns and equipment. Stand by ready for orders. Airmen to go on route marches by FLIGHTS.
ALL FLIGHTS warned of possible operation. Preparations begin – stocktaking of equipment, guns etc. Conference of FLIGHT COMMANDERS with COMMANDING OFFICER, arrangements made for hardening of Flight personnel. 1 vehicle returned by 2906 SQUADRON. 13 airmen now sick in SQUADRON, possibly evacuated from ISLAND. "A" FLIGHT ran rifle shooting contest as part of training.
2nd. Vehicle returned by 2906 Squadron.
"C" Flight went on 5 Mile route march. More ammunition was distributed to all FLIGHTS. COMMANDING OFFICER visited W/C. GOULD at SAN FRANCESCO. F/LT. WHITBREAD of R.A.F. REGIMENT HEADQUARTERS visited SQUADRON to see ADJUTANT.
"A" Flight went on route march. COMMANDING OFFICER visited W/C. GOULD at "B" WING HEADQUARTERS.
"B" Flight went on route march. A visit to the WELFARE OFFICER, D.A.F., at CATANIA by the COMMANDING OFFICER and ADJUTANT obtained cigarettes, magazines other comforts and the promise of a wireless set. P/O. M. WILDEN admitted to hospital suffering from malaria.
Administrative Instructions for future operations contained in RHQDAFAF/S.1062/6/ORG dated 26th August, 1943 were received by this unit. Efforts were made to complete anti-mosquito equipment by

2862 (LAA) Sqn – Operational at Agnone Landing Ground

Nothing to Report.
F/O Steen discharged from 239 Wing Hospital.
A general overhaul of all Squadron Transport.
Nothing to report. F/O Steen admitted to S.S.Q. 329 Wing.
All guns were tested and found to be in working order.
The following extract received from R.H.Q., Desert Air Force:- "Casualties are occurring to men and equipment of our Forces through missiles which are not self-destructive; shells fired from 20 mm. Hispano guns operated by A/A Squadrons of the R.A.F. Regiment are in this category. It has been decided to place certain restrictions on the operational use of weapons firing non-self-destroying missiles. This directive outlines the broad policy as it concerns A/A Squadrons of the R.A.F. Regiment. From the above it will be seen that the role of the L.A.A. Squadrons is very limited without the use of self-destructive shells.
Nothing to report.
Squadron Leader W.E. Sheil summoned to H.Q. R.A.F.R. The following appointments were made in the Squadron:- F/O. Steen. -------------- Sports Officer. F/O. Odgers. ------------ Messing Officer. F/O. Benthrone. ---------- Officer i/c Fire. Instruction on prevention firefighting given by this Officer.
Nothing to report.

2857 (LAA) Sqn – Operational at Scordia Landing Ground

Squadron Leader Chapman complaining of sickness, but is carrying on.
Rumoured that 8th Army have finally cleared the enemy from island, but not definite news.
Squadron Leader Chapman admitted to 30 Military Field Hospital, with slight attack of Malaria.

OPERATION 'HUSKY' – the Sicilian Campaign 1943

Enemy have evacuated Sicily, where to now?
Sickness is about 19% of the Squadron chiefly Malaria cases. Am of the opinion that Mosquito nets should have been issued on the ship before disembarking, in actual fact we only managed to obtain 7 days after landing. Other Squadrons who arrived on this island have I believe about the same percentage of sickness.
A/C Tobin discharged from 25 M.F.H. and arrived back to this Squadron after hitch hiking several hours in a very weak condition, if we had been advised of his discharge, it would have been possible to have arranged transport to have collected him.
Squadron Leader Chapman does not appear to be making much progress, am rather concerned at his condition.
No activity for some days now, the weather is still very hot.
Training the men on various weapons to relive the monotony of gun crew duties.
Rained for a few minutes but sufficient enough to make the tracks very hard going for the D.R.'s. Much cooler. Inventories of all stores taken. Inspection of vehicles by M.T. Officers.
Squadron Leader Chapman returned from 30. M.F.H. but still far from well. Regimental concert party is being organised by F/Lt. Tiffin they are to give their first show at Regimental H.Q. Aug 28th.
Nothing of interest to report.
Squadron Commander has now completely recovered from his illness. General health of Squadron has very much improved.
To give some relaxation to the men, the C.O. has laid down that men off duty can in turn go swimming near Catania under the supervision of an Officer.
First R.A.F.R. concert given at 2855 Sdn H.Q. A good performance which was much enjoyed by all ranks.
Nothing to report.
Some air activity last night over what appeared to be Syracuse.
The last day of the month and despite the rather bad run of sickness which we suffered at the beginning, a position which has very much improved, the spirit and morale of the Squadron is very high.

OPERATION 'HUSKY' – the Sicilian Campaign 1943

2859 (LAA) Sqn – Operational at San Francesco Landing Ground

Normal Squadron Operational Routine.
A Roman Catholic service was held on the Squadron site at 09.30hrs. LAC. BATTERHAM was admitted to Hospital and his case has been diagnosed as Malaria.
Normal Squadron Operational Routine.
Normal Squadron Operational Routine. Squadron Concert Party gave its 3rd concert, and was well received by a larger audience then hitherto, which included many Officers and airmen from neighbouring Squadrons.
Normal Squadron Operational Routine. A Church of England Service was held on the Squadron site at 19.00hrs. An unfortunate accident occurred this afternoon when Sgt. DAWSON picked up a round of enemy 20mm. ammunition which exploded in his hands resulting in lacerations of hands and chest. He was admitted to No.30 M.F.H. Disciplinary action will be taken against this airman in view of repeated warnings in regard to picking up of objects lying on the ground.
LAC. SKINNER who was admitted to Hospital on 28.7.43 and transferred to Tripoli, returned to the Unit today. Normal Squadron Operational Routine.
Normal Squadron Operational Routine.
65 Airmen arrived from Replacement Pool and are to be accommodated with this Unit until disposal instructions have been received from Headquarters. Training programme commenced. LAC. ALLEN (932) was admitted to Hospital today and his case has been diagnosed as Malaria.
Operational Routine and Training Programme carried out. The weekly concert was held this afternoon instead of this evening. Artists from Units in the vicinity entertained a large audience, and were well received. Sgt. MILLS was admitted to Hospital this afternoon and his case has been diagnosed as Malaria.
Operational Routine and Training Programme carried out. The Squadron Leader heard the charge against 1256222 Sgt. DAWSON,

F. and reprimanded him. No Religious Service was held today owing to a severe storm.
Operational Routine and Training Programme carried out. The 65 airmen who have been accommodated with the Squadron awaiting disposal proceeded to No.2855 Squadron for training. 2. 3 Ton Bedfords from 2857 Sqdn., 1. 3 Ton Bedford from 2906 Sqdn., 1. 3 Ton Dodge from 2925 Sqdn. & 1. 15 cwt vehicle from 2904 Sqdn. Were loaned this Unit.
Operational Routine and Training Programme carried out.

2925 (LAA) Sqn – Operational at Lentini East Landing Ground

The Commanding Officer visited Rear H.Q., D.A.F. and informed P.M.O. of RUNDLE's death. P.M.O. had not received a casualty signal from 4 C.C.S. and had not received his personal effects. Another visit was made to 4 C.C.S. and a Burial Certificate obtained.
The personnel from the Squadron attended concert given by Regimental Concert Party at 2855 Squadron. Officers attended an "At Home" at 2855 Squadron after the show.
At about 15.00 hours a severs rainstorm broke over LENTINI rendering the L.G. (W) unserviceable and making all tracks almost impassable to wheeled traffic. "B" and "C" Flights, who were living in tents, suffered considerable damage from the water, tents being washed away and all bedding and equipment getting soaked. Headquarters was more fortunate being in a farmhouse. The gun posts were feet deep in water which turned to liquid mud as the water soaked in. The rain cleared up about 17.00hrs but there was insufficient sun to dry out the ground that night.
The Unit was engaged most of the day in cleaning sites, drying out equipment and cleaning guns after yesterday's storm. The Unit played 2859 Squadron at Soccer on San Francesco airfield in the evening, the result being a win for the Squadron by 2 goals to nil.

OPERATION 'HUSKY' – the Sicilian Campaign 1943

2864 (LAA) Sqn – Operational at Palmero Aerodrome

Completion of unloading of equipment and transfer to aerodrome.
O.C. accompanied S/Ldr Symons on a reconnaissance of aerodrome.
Conference with Lt.Col. Coward and Major Levine (52nd Fighter Group) Major Ripley (1st A.D.W.) and S/Ldr Symons when the latter disclosed his scheme for guards, patrols and defence of the aerodrome which was approved in principle. It was agreed that subject to co-ordination the local A.A. Commanders this Unit should mount 20 m.m. A.A. Guns for manning in event of an attack.
O.C. made further reconnaissance of aerodrome accompanied by 2 i/c and Flight Commanders. Areas to be patrolled and guarded allocated to respective Flights. (A short Defence Scheme is to be prepared in which these will be specified in detail)
Guards and patrols started. No.3 Flight moved to Main Guard Room at S.W. of aerodrome.
No.1 Flight pitched tents site S.E. of aerodrome. No.2 Flight pitched tents site N.E. of aerodrome.
Work started of blocking of holes in walls and closing large gaps in wiring of perimeter, which it is anticipated will take several weeks. Static guards at Main entrance to airfield taken over, at the request of Major Levine (52nd Fighter Group).
C.O. saw O.C. "E" Bty. 62nd C.A.A. (Coastal A.A.) who are manning A.A. defences at Palermo and aerodrome concerning mounting of 20 m.m. Isotta guns by this Unit and it was left to discretion of this Unit as to most suitable sites.
O.C. visited 62nd C.A.A. Regimental H.Q. and obtained the approval of the Officer Commanding that Regt. To the manning of A.A. Guns by this Unit in the event of an attack. It was arranged that this Squadron should be linked to G.O.R.
Visit to this Unit by Wing Commander Abbott, N.A.C.A.F. and S/Ldr Symons.
No occurrence of importance on these days.
Air Raid Alert. Raid directed against Dock area of Palermo only.
Major General Lord Rennell, Chief Civil Affairs Officer, in the Palermo Sector, accompanied by his A.D.C. Major Pirie, visited the

OPERATION 'HUSKY' – the Sicilian Campaign 1943

unit and requested O.C. of this Unit, as Senior R.A.F. Officer in this Sector so far as was known, to undertake responsibility for discipline of all R.A.F. personnel in the area and the American Provost-Marshall was to be informed accordingly. He also requested to be notified of all R.A.F. Units in the area as soon as possible. The General later visited the Squadron mess.
O.C. visited Lt. Col. Burch, Provost-Marshall Palermo, and informed him of Major General Lord Rennell's decision.
No occurrence of importance on these dates.
O.C. received orders to attend Major General Lord Rennell of Rodd at Base Operations Room Palermo aerodrome immediately.
O.C. attended Major General Lord Rennell as directed. Others present were Major General House and Major General Cannon (?) both of U.S. Army and Lt.Col. Howell, U.S. Army – Station Commander. Personal orders were given to O.C. this Unit by Major General Lord Rennell to the following effect:- At 17.00 hours today an ITALIAN aircraft would land on Palermo Airfield under Allied Fighter Escort. The aircraft would be met and the Officers taken by automobile to his residence under arrangements made by him. Italian O.R's in the aircraft would be accommodated under cover and out of sight with this Unit. They were to be allowed access to their aircraft but were to have no contact with any civilians or Allied personnel other than this Unit. They were to be well treated but kept under escort during the whole of their stay. This Unit would mount a continuous guard on the aircraft and would allow no-one to touch or inspect the aircraft. The aircraft itself to be concealed from view so far as possible. The continuous guard on the aircraft to consist of two men on guard at all times.
Instructions received from 62 C.A.A. Regimental H.Q. (U.S. Army) that no A.A. guns would open fire between 15.00 and 19.00 hrs.
A three engine Savoia Marchetti landed at Palermo aerodrome and was met by Major General Lord Rennell accompanied by his A.D.C., Air Commodore Cross, A.O.C. 242 Group, in company with an Air Vice Marshall and another Air Commodore, were present – also Lt. Col. Howell, Station Commander. A large crowd quickly assembled but all other persons were excluded from the airfield by a guard provided by

this Unit. Major General Lord Rennell was accompanied to the aeroplane by O.C. and 2nd i/c this Unit. One passenger was conducted to the General's car. O.C. this Unit entered the aeroplane which was taxied by the crew to a dispersal point across the aerodrome, where it was placed under guard provided by this Unit, who was already in position. The guard was commanded by F/O. J.A. Henson and a continual guard of 4 airmen was mounted. The aeroplane was covered with tarpaulins and camouflage nets. The crew were conducted to Headquarters No.2 Flight and placed in the custody of F/O. Wright, who retained them in his own quarters.

A Capitain E.P.N. De Haan accompanied by an Italian civilian reported to O.C. and demanded that the Italian plane leave immediately, i.e. at 13.00hrs, with the Italian as passenger. He stated that he was acting under orders of a General Beetle-Smith. He also requested permission to see the crew. Under orders already received the latter request was declined. O.C. immediately saw Major Hegele, The Station Adjutant, to ascertain if orders had been received to release the plane, and explained that the guard could not be removed or access granted to the crew unless such orders had been received. No orders had been received and it was decided that O.C. should visit Major General Lord Rennell in Palermo immediately. O.C. was unable to find the General either at his Offices or Private Residence or anyone competent to discuss the matter and after leaving a note at this Office, again reported to Major Negele.

Lt. Col. Coward, O.C. 52nd Fighter Group, then interviewed Captain De Haan and explained that as the latter had no written authority and no orders had been received for the plane to leave, it could not do so.

Lt. Col. Spofforth reported to Station Commander that he had Major General Lord Rennell's orders that the plane would depart at 16.00hrs with another passenger whom the General would bring with him at that time. These orders were explained to Captain De Hann. Orders were given by O.C. this Unit for the crew to be brought to the plane in readiness.

Major General Lord Rennell arrived accompanied by one passenger and requested to see O.C. who explained position to him.

The General accompanied his passenger and the other passenger

brought by Captain De Haan to the plane which then departed.
The guard provided by this Unit was dismounted.
No occurrence of importance.

OPERATION 'HUSKY' – the Sicilian Campaign 1943

No.2859 Sqn Operational Orders – San Francesco Landing Ground

APPENDIX 'A'

OPERATION ORDER No.1.   MOST SECRET

     By

Squadron Leader A.J.B. Vidlor   Copy No. 10.

Commanding No. 2859 A.A. Sqdn. R.A.F. Regiment

R.A.F. Station, San Francesco.

INFORMATION.   Enemy Troops unknown.

                    Own Troops.

                    No.2859 A.A. Sqdn. R.A.F.R. 8 Officers, 151 Other Ranks.

                    Two Troops of No.225 Batt. L.A.A. 6 Officers, 160 Other Ranks.

                    South African Air Force, No.40 Squadron –

                    220 Officers and Other Ranks. (May be available but cannot be included in the scheme).

                    One troop Heavy A.A. in support. "A" Troop. 17th Battery 1st. H.A.A. Regt. R.A.

INTENTION.   The Airfield and approaches of R.A.F. Station SAN FRANCESCO, Map Reference: 82:52, Sheet 273/1. Italy 1/50,000 – Catania, will be denied from the enemy at all costs.

METHOD.   "G" and "K" Troop of No.225 Batt. L.A.A. are deployed to a depth of 200 yards North, West and South sides of the Airfield, and the 12 Fun Positions and two troop Headquarters will, in the event of attach by ground troops, form strong points of their positions. "G" Troop will hold ground Map Ref: 837550 Sheet 273 Pt.1. "K" Troop cover road and river approach Map Reference 325534 Sheet 273 Pt.1.

                    The duty Gunners of the R.A.F.R. will continue their normal role of Light A.A. and Nos. 2 & 3 will take up positions as riflemen to protect the Gun Positions.

                    The Headquarters Hispano will be manned by Gunners available in H.Q. Flight.

                    Anti-tank rifles will be placed in position when available.

                    All personnel not on Gunnery Duties will proceed to fixed positions "X" and "Y" East of Squadron Headquarters with personal arms.

Two Bren Guns will be manned in the machine gun pits. This force will be commanded by O.C. No.2859 Squadron.

ADMINISTRATION.

The Main Ground force will be commanded by the O.C. Squadron, or in his absence, the next senior Officer.

A.A. Defences will be commanded by their respective Flight Commanders and 2ns in command and Squadron Adjutant will proceed to areas "X" and "Y" in the locality.

No.2859 Sqn Map of Gun Positions – San Francesco Landing Ground

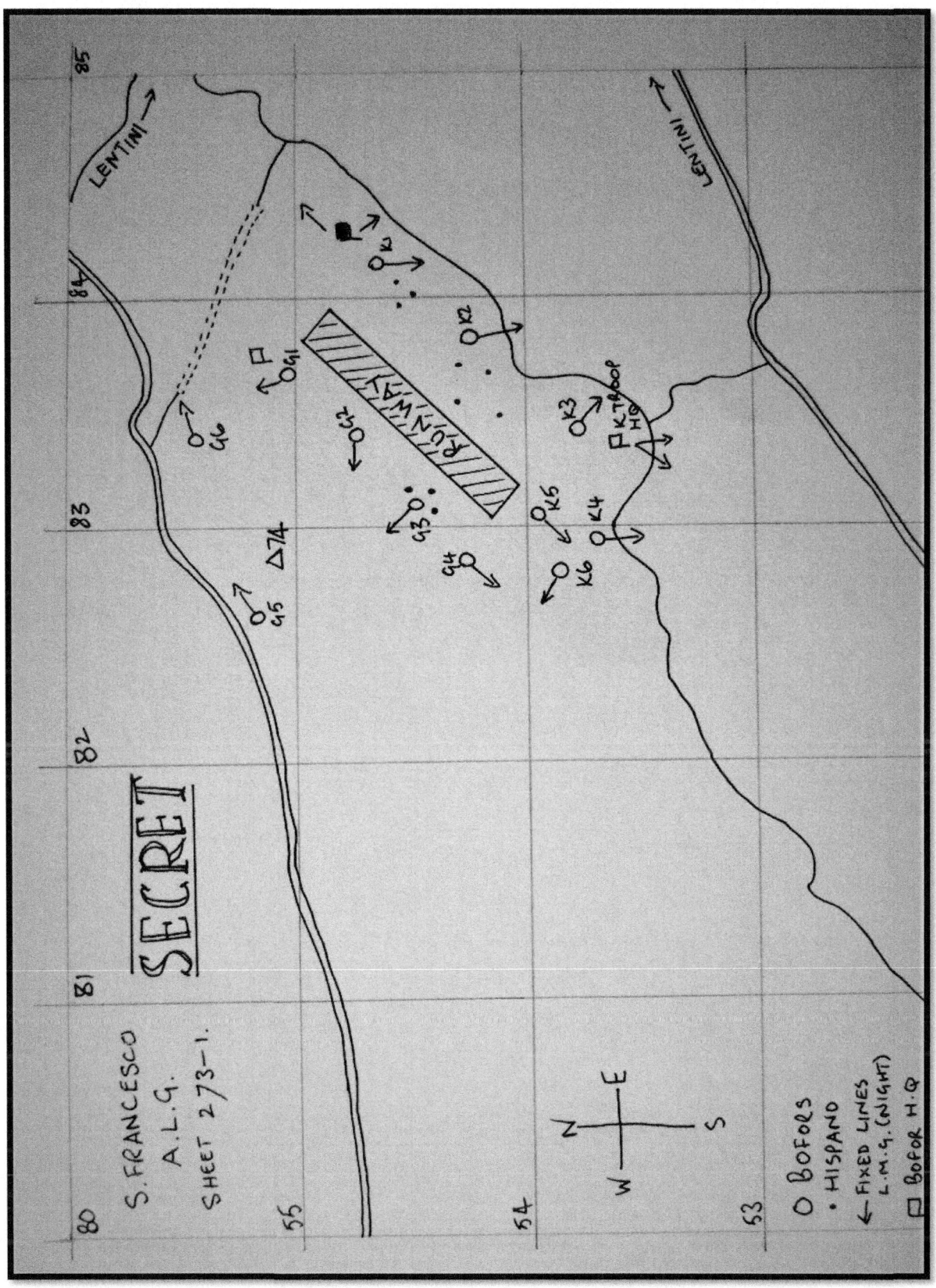

(Author copy of original sketch map)

OPERATION 'HUSKY' – the Sicilian Campaign 1943

No.2859 Sqn Standing Order for Special A.A. Course

APPENDIX "B"

STANDING ORDERS FOR SPECIAL A.A. COURSE (HISPANO).

SAN FRANCESCO AIRFIELD.

1. DISCIPLINE. A high standing of discipline will be maintained at all times and NCO Instructors are responsible for their own party.

2. BOUNDS. All towns in the surrounding districts are out of bounds.

3. PASSES. No passes will be granted to personnel on course under any circumstances and therefore personnel will not proceed from camp site except for washing purposes.

4. MEALS. A programme will be displayed on the notice board and this will be strictly adhered to.

5. SICK PARADE. Personnel reporting sick will report to first aid tent at 07.30 hours strict disciplinary action will be taken against any person malingering.

6. SKILL ARMS. All personal weapons will be cleaned before morning parade and will be kept in possession of owner except when proceeding to the river for washing when they will be handed in to Squadron Armoury for safe custody.

7. SQUADRON ROUTINE ORDERS. All personnel attached to 2859 Squadron for this course will read Squadron Routine Orders daily.

8. GUARDS. All personnel will provide a picquet on this site for the duration of the course and a roster will be prepared by the C.I.
Squadron Guard Orders will be read over to the guard by N.C.O. i/c picquet before the guard commences duty.

9. AMMUNITION. Personal ammo. Will be kept in safe custody of airmen concerned and magazines will not be charged except on an order given by an officer or N.C.O.

10. N.A.A.F.I. Airmen om=n course from other Squadrons will under no circumstance be permitted to purchase goods from Squadron N.A.A.F.I. in view of the fact that no supplies are obtained from N.A.A.F.I. on their behalf. Cigarettes however,

will be drawn from D.I.D. if possible and issued to all airmen.

11. <u>CIVILIANS</u>. All civilians will be ordered off the camp site and no purchases will be made from them.

These orders will be read by all course personnel prior to commencement of course.

Squadron Leader, Commanding,

<u>No. 2859 Squadron, R.A.F. Regiment.</u>

OPERATION 'HUSKY' – the Sicilian Campaign 1943

No.2859 Sqn Special A.A. Course – timetable

APPENDIX 'B'

SPECIAL A.A. COURSE (HISPANO).

SAN FRANCESCO AIRFIELD, SHEET 273/1. MAP REF: 839545.

	1st. Day.	2nd. Day.	3rd. Day.	4th. Day.
08.00hrs	1st. Parade & Inspection.	1st. Parade & Inspection.	1st. Parade & Inspection.	1st. Parade & Inspection.
08.30hrs	Introductory talk by S/Ldr. Vidler.	Names of parts C.S.A.D. Mounting.	Stoppages.	Load guns on lorries.
09.00hrs	Allocation of Instructors			Proceed to Firing Range.
09.15hrs	Description of Hispano 20mm. Gun.	Gun Drill	Gun Drill	
10.00hrs	BREAK	BREAK	BREAK	
10.15hrs	Description of C.S.A.D. Mounting	Mechanism.	Sighting.	
11.00hrs	Gun Drill, Demonstration & Practice.	Practical stripping of gun.	Description of Ammo.	
12.00hrs	DINNER.	DINNER.	DINNER.	
13.30hrs	Parade.	Parade.	Parade.	
13.45hrs	Names of parts Hispano Gun	Points before firing.	Points before firing.	
14.30hrs	Mechanism.	Practical stripping of mounting.	General Revision.	
15.15hrs	Gun Drill.	Gun Drill.	Efficiency Test.	
16.00hrs	BREAK.	BREAK.	BREAK.	
16.15hrs	General Revision & Questions.	General Revision & Questions.	Efficiency Test. (continued)	
17.00hrs	TEA.	TEA.	TEA.	

About the Author

After serving 10 years with the R.A.F. Regiment (the Regiment), and leaving in the early 1990s, I settled in Oxfordshire, and for more than 25 years have worked in Local Government. My passion for the Regiment, and in particular, the people who have served, has always been strong. After recently finishing my Master's, my thirst for knowledge remained and having read the main published books on the Regiment, I decided to delve deeper into understanding its early evolution and the men who had served.

It was while I was writing a book on the Squadrons, Men and Equipment of the R.A.F. Regiment 1942 – 45, that I realised I had significant gaps in my understanding of early unit structures and their evolution. So, I decided to spend a day at The National Archives to find out more.

That day at The National Archives, looking through the Operational Record Books (the records) of several units, introduced to a wealth of information and 'gems' that brought to life, what really happened in those informative years.

This book is the result of many more days at the National Archives and the bringing together of several different strands of information. I hope you enjoy this slice of history.

Other books by the Author

Operation 'Torch' and the North African Campaign 1942- 43 Part 1 – eBook July 2017

Operation 'Torch' and the North African Campaign 1942- 43 Part 2 – eBook August 2017

Operation 'Torch' and the North African Campaign 1942- 43 – Paperback August 2017

Planned books for this operation and campaign series

The Mediterranean Campaign

Operation 'Overlord' and the North West European Campaign

Operation 'Diver' and the Campaign against the 'V' Rockets

Bibliography

Batt. Keith (Gp Capt), *'The RAF Regiment - A Short History'*, 40th Anniversary Edition, 1982

Oliver. M. Kingsley (Gp Capt), *'The RAF Regiment at War 1942 - 1946'*, 2002

Oliver. M. Kingsley (Gp Capt), *'Through Adversity – The History of the Royal Air Force Regiment 1942 - 1992'*, 1997

Zaloga. J. Steven, *'SICILY 1943 - The debut of Allied joint operations'*, 2013

Operational Record Books (The National Archives)

AIR 29/84 - **2744 Field Squadron**

AIR 29/116 – **2855/ 2856 L.A.A. Squadrons**

AIR 29/117 - **2857/ 2858/ 2858 L.A.A. Squadrons**

AIR 29/118 – **2862/ 2864 L.A.A. Squadrons**

AIR 29/129 – **2904/ 2906 Field Squadrons**

AIR 29/133 – **2925 L.A.A. Squadron**

AIR 29/120 – **RAF Regiment Squadrons 2852 – 2867 Appendices only**

AIR 29/130 - **RAF Regiment Squadrons 2900 – 2909 Appendices only**

AIR29/135 - **RAF Regiment Squadrons 2924 – 2935 Appendices only**

Printed in Great Britain
by Amazon